The Ultimate Guide to Self-Healing,
Personal Growth and Life Management

Wisdom Rising II

PURPLE HAZE PRESS

by *Vaishāli*

Purple Haze Press books can be ordered through booksellers or by visiting www.PurpleHazePress.com or www.PurpleV.com or by contacting:

Purple Haze Press
2430 Vanderbilt Beach Road, #108
PMB #167
Naples, FL 34109

First Printing, 2012

Library of Congress Control Number: 2012937680

Others books by Vaishali:
You Are What You Love©,
The You Are What You Love Playbook,
Wisdom Rising

ISBN 978-1-935183-09-9
epublish ISBN 978-1-935183-10-5
epdf ISBN 978-1-935183-14-3

1. New Age   2. Spirituality   3. Non-fiction
4. Love   5. Natural Health   6. Self-Help

This book is dedicated to:

Cameron, Courtney and Marla

Thank you for having the courage to share the journey with me.

Every book is the gift of many talents and sources of inspiration and support. Special thanks to:

Aime and Steve McCrory: http://www.thebusinessmuse.com/,

Brian and Robin Narelle: http://www.narellecreative.net/,

Jeffrey K. Bedrick: http://jeffreykbedrick.com/,

Darlene Swanson: http://www.van-garde.com

and Pela Tomasello.

I would also like to thank all those supportive and caring loved ones: Joe & Janet Cosgrove, Jennifer Scalia, Karen Kaye, Ruthie Biafora, Cameron and Davindia Steele, Yvonne Mitchelson, Michael Monteleone, Dr. Marilyn Chernoff and Nancy from the The Healing Center, Milton Edwards, Jill Lawrence, Nance Parry, Gia Scott, Rev. Phil, Rosemary Thomas, Maxine Chavez, Judi Gifford, John and Shelly Misiorowski, Carolyn and Marcus Blakemore, Alfred Cormier and Lisa Timmons, Phyllis King and of course, Miss Grace and Miss Bliss.

Table of Contents

Mind

Body

Spirit

Mind

2012

Are You Ready?

*E*verywhere I go I hear conversations — rumblings about 2012. But what *exactly* is this 2012 thing all about? Let me start out by qualifying our examination of it: until the imminent date Dec. 21, 2012 (or 11:11 GMT), becomes a present moment reality, all conversations about this topic are merely conjecture and speculation. Nothing is known for sure. With that said, here is the meat of the 2012 phenomenon.

Some time around the third through the ninth centuries AD, the Ancient Mayans, located in what we now recognize as Central Mexico south to the Yucatán, Guatemala, Belize, El Salvador and some of Western Honduras created a calendar. The Mayan calendar is just one among a very impressive list of things the Mayan civilization developed, such as the most advanced Pre-Columbian written language, mathematical and astronomical systems, exquisite works of art and outstanding architectural achievements. Clearly the Mayans were not a group of slackers, lacking in imagination, creativity or sheer brilliance.

Although the 2012 debate rages around just the Mayan calendar, I mention these other accomplishments simply to offer a greater context and validation of the creators of this work. Unlike our contemporary 365-day Gregorian calendar, the Mayan version was more like a collection of calendars based on many cycles and cycles within cycles, and how they related to other cycles and almanacs. Much has been written about the many elements and complexities of the Mayan calendar, but for our purpose we are going to focus on a 26,000-year cycle which the Mayan calendar predicts will end on Dec 21, 2012, thus starting a brand new 26,000-year cycle.

Here is what we know about the Winter Solstice of 2012. We will be moving from the Piscean Age to the Aquarian Age. Over the course of a year the Sun moves through every house in the zodiac. In a 26,000-year cycle the planet moves through each of the 12 zodiac ages, each age being a little over 2,000 years long. There is also a relationship between the Sun and the Milky Way (the Galaxy *not* the candy bar). Once every 26,000 years the Sun conjuncts the intersection of the Milky Way and the plane of our solar system, thus putting us in alignment with our galaxy. This marks the end of the Earth's 26,000-year roundtrip tour of the Milky Way and the start of a fresh 26,000-year journey.

Another way to visualize it would be this: I like to re-set my car's trip odometer every time I stop and refuel my car. So I push the button, and all the numbers return to zero, thus beginning the recording on a new cycle of movement. My car does not come to an end; I do not come to an end; and God knows gas prices do not come to an end. I am simply recording and marking the beginning of a new cycle of movement.

So far, none of this sounds too scary or "airy fairy", right? So why is there all this end of the world talk associated with this 2012 cosmic, inter-galactic odometer re-setting? Historically speaking, people have not always responded to the unknown in the most healthy and predictable of ways, and this event seems to be no exception to that rule. Add to that something as mysterious and open to interpretation as the Mayan calendar and you have a veritable confluence of volatile reactions.

The end of the Mayan calendar may have some "outer world" implications. The scientific community has been pointing out for some time that the planet may be ready to shift magnetic poles. When exactly that will happen no one really knows for certain. Some predict by 2012. What that means is that the magnet North Pole will become the South Pole and visa versa. This has happened in the history of the Earth before, but never during a post-industrial time. No one really knows what the global repercussions will be. But it does seem obvious that mass communication: radio, television, cell phones, computers will on longer work after that magnet pole shift occurs as the electro-magnetic spectrum will have been turned on its head. With no cell phone reception or email, it is easy to see why many might call that the end of the world.

There is also a scientific prediction of increased plate tectonic activity, meaning more earthquakes and volcanic activity, which in turn could produce more devastating tsunamis like the kinds we saw in Indonesia and Japan. There is even an emphasis on the probability of increased freak weather patterns - more frequent and violent hurricanes and tornadoes. And these are just a few of the "outer world" implications.

There is also an "inner world" interpretation of this new age cycle that views this event as the dawning of a new age of con-sciousness, not cataclysmic global trauma. The idea is that this new cycle is about a rapid expansion of the collective human consciousness that will have evolved by 2012 much like the hundredth monkey theory. The hundredth monkey theory is based on experiments done with monkeys and sweet potatoes. The potatoes, not indigenous to the monkey's diet, were dumped on a beach. One monkey figured out the potatoes made for a more enjoyable dining experience if washed first. Once that monkey taught one hundred other monkeys to wash their potatoes, the collective consciousness of the monkey population, not just limited to that island, immediately shared the epiphany. This experiment showed that even monkeys, nowhere near where the tests were conducted washed sweet potatoes dumped on their beach, as if they had known this behavior their entire lives. That's why the minute you have a computer or any "advanced technology" problem, the first thing you do is contact any 12 year old. (It's not that they are any smarter than you, it could be that you're just the 99th monkey.)

For many, the Spiritual promise of 2012 is the heralding of a golden age of a higher evolved awareness. A time where the collective consciousness of the planet is experienced as more united and unfettered by the previous Piscean Age of brutality and self-absorbed arrogance. A final, globally shared gestalt that all of human life is deeply and permanently interconnected. As long as one group of people are struggling and suffering, we are *all* struggling and suffering. An ultimate awakening to a quality of consciousness that integrates us all, rather than separates us. A time when the power and worldwide abundance will flow from the hands of the few back into the hands of the many. An Age of planetary equalization. Think of it as an Earth encompassing affirmative action program - only this one would actually work.

Here is the bottom line... whether you gravitate toward the "outer world" interpretation or the "inner world" vision of 2012, change is what life is all about. Tomorrow is promised to no one; the time to practice mastery over change is now. Be comfortable with change. Invite it into your life with an optimistic attitude and open heart. Whatever 2012 brings, change is guaranteed and inevitable. If you are the kind of person who resists change, likes everything to stay the same, then you probably respond to life challenges by contracting back into your comfort zone, instead of manifesting an out-of-the-box reaction. This means you will not be comfortable in a rapidly expanding and changing world.

Here is what you can start doing right now to prepare:

- Practice doing things differently, even if it is just driving a different route than usual, watching a different television show, eating something unusual, dressing out of your traditional order, or installing the toilet paper over instead of under.

- Shake things up! Acclimate yourself to a climate of change and expansion. Be at ease and non-resistant to change and growth, no matter how inconvenient the circumstances.

- Give the pathways of your mind an opportunity to create new connections. Embrace the unexpected as a learning gift, and as another occasion to empower your relationship with change. Be the change you wish to see, as Gandhi so eloquently phrased it.

- Make change an energy you thrive on rather than

a force you defy. Let change be the teacher and instructor of the moment. Allow a willingness of flourishing change to emerge organically in your life.

We came to the planet Earth to learn, to grow and to share more love. Whether 2012 ushers in radical physical Earth shifts or revelations of consciousness, relaxing into the flow of the ever-changing "what is" will always be relevant and serving. Transformation has always exerted its presence on the Earth and that will not disappear no matter what 2012 brings. Imagine the arrival of 2012 as an invitation to liberate what restrains and inhibits you, as an opportunity to grow in ways you had not previously considered. This would be a wise and unconditionally useful choice. That way no matter what life, 2012, or one hundred monkeys throw at you, you'll be ready, resilient, primed, change-friendly and self-actualizing. Be sure to put *that* on your calendar. And don't forget to pick up your new 26,000-year calendar before the office supply stores run out. I heard they're only $50,000.

How To Own & Operate The Human Experience

*W*ouldn't it be great if life came with an owner's manual and a warranty with a double your money back guarantee of complete satisfaction? That would be the ideal fantasy – no suffering, no fuss, no muss, no headaches, no assembly required. However, life does not come with any legally binding contracts of unconditional happiness. What most us here have already realized is that life is not meant to be a success only journey.

So how do we make the most of our time here on Earth? How do we learn to move forward when we have no idea of what direction life is taking us? These great and classic questions require great and classic wisdom. Over two thousand years ago in ancient Greece the quintessential philosopher, Socrates, said it best when he uttered those immortal words, "The unexamined life is not worth living." To this day no one has improved upon this basic truth for owning and operating the human experience. So, let's start here.

No one can live an examined life without developing a mature, healthy and functional relationship with his or her own mind… with consciousness. Consciousness is something we are never without – no vacations, no coffee breaks not even death. If you

11

are asleep, then you are experiencing dreaming consciousness. Even if you are in a coma or heavily medicated, you are still experiencing some form of consciousness even if it is a trance-like state of existence. Consciousness is inescapable. Being *aware* is the reflexive action of conscious examination. And examining our lives by being aware of what we are giving our attention to can be a shallow and fragile relationship, as well as a state from which we are easily and frequently distracted.

Living an examined life denotes paying attention to what you are doing with your mind. It is about knowing when your attention has wandered off to a self-sabotaging or self-loathing place that is damaging, life diminishing, and bringing it back from these distractions. The mind is like an undisciplined child running off and creating havoc with its unfocused energy. This is why, for thousands of years, meditation has been practiced and taught as a means of becoming self-actualizing. Try this awareness experiment: just take one day out of your life and write down what you find yourself frequently giving your attention to. Take note of what inner dialogue and stories your consciousness gravitates or constantly returns to. Notice what non-life sustaining habitual crevices your mind repeatedly slips into. Most of us are extremely loyal and faithful to what we give our attention to, even to the point of being grossly repetitive or successful in producing only one result: unhappiness.

The ultimate purpose of living an examined life is to make your mind your best friend and most supportive ally, instead of your worst enemy - an undermining, toxic, intimate relationship. To begin to determine how friendly you are with your own mind, just acknowledge how often you tell yourself something harsh or deliberately hurtful… something that you would be reluctant to articulate to even your least favorite person on the planet. The truth is, if there is one relationship you need to make a loving and reliably comfortable place, it has to be your own mind. After all if there is one consistent element in life, it is that you will always be in relationship with yourself. That will never change. And, since no one knows how to "do it to you" like you, whether that is extending a patient voice of comfort and inspiration or giving voice to the critical, sharp-tongued inner harpy, it is a intimate dynamic you are destined to live with in an up-close and deeply personal way. You know you have the comprehensive capacity for being both self-supporting and self-deprecating. Which quality is the one most likely to rule your life? The one you practice most frequently giving your attention to, of course.

How much of your attention goes into worrying and torturing yourself compulsively with thoughts about events you have absolutely no control over? Have you ever noticed that over 90% of the time the things you focus on that create such misery and stress in your life never come to pass? These are the most common ways we relate to our own mind in a most insidiously adverse fashion. Then we heighten the damage by faithfully poking the sensitive spots over and over again, as if that ever improved the situation!

Most of us are very adept at sleepwalking through life. We allow our attention to go into an autopilot type of functioning mode. Whenever we are not conscious of what we are giving our attention to, the unconscious mind takes over. It continually regurgitates the undigested, unreleased inner waste that we have not recognized as useless and fraudulent. It obsesses over whatever we have not consciously chosen to separate from. This is why we say or do such stupid, embarrassing things when we are not paying attention. Because the conscious mind is asleep at the wheel, and the unconscious mind has taken over.

Making your mind your friend is how you raise yourself from an infantile, self-indulgent form of semi-consciousness to a mature, disciplined and balanced experience of self-awareness. The interior process of raising your mind is very similar to the exterior process of raising a child. Every time you find yourself giving your attention to something limiting, self-defeating, mean-spirited, critical... STOP! Then like a dutiful parent you tirelessly remove that myopic focus of attention from your mental grip and then refocus it on what is healthy, expansive, productive and freeing.

For example, replaying the thought that you do not have enough money is like a child who keeps putting their hand in the fire. Fixating on that "not enough" story that "I am lacking" has never solved a single problem. It has yet to add additional dollars to your bank account, put more cash in your pocket, support you in feeling better about yourself, actualize your highest potential or help you sleep at night. Quite the contrary. Adjusting your mental lens to focusing on the scarcity issues attracts feelings of hopelessness, loss of power, disposable and unloved. You become a victim. It has inflamed your level of suffering and left you feeling physically and emotionally burned out. Like a child that has not yet predictably learned that putting their hand on the stove is how they get burned, unbroken loyalty to that line of self-inflicted, limited awareness repeatedly scars, disfigures and deeply pains you.

Don't get me wrong, I am not advocating for denial, self-delusion or burying one's head in the sand. What I am pointing out is that there are many, many things that happen in life that you have no control over. At the end of the day, you may not be able to control if you get that dream job, if a loan or that house sale goes through or even if you are going to have a bad hair day, but what you *always* do have control over is what you give your attention to and how you feel about that. So, instead of everything in your life revolving around the notion, the minute details of where you do not have enough, what if you shifted your field of attention to being grateful for the money you do have, the health you do have, the loving, caring relationships you do have? At the end of the day would the exterior details of your life be any different? Maybe. Maybe not. But here is the essential difference: you would feel more comfortable in your own skin with an increased sense of relaxation about your experience of life. If all you *do* have power over is how you feel at the end of the day and what quality of life you are actively creating, what would that be worth to you? That is the payoff in making you mind your friend.

If feeling better about yourself is not sufficient motivation, let me point out the mind/body connection. The body responds in a powerful way to what you give your attention to. You do not need all the scientific research that proves visualizing the body's immune system destroying viruses, bacteria, even cancer cells produces healthy, revitalizing results to understand this. You can prove this to yourself. Notice how you feel when you think about something in your life you deeply regret or something you value that is now gone, whether that is a loved one, your dream job or financial investments that evaporated into thin air. Now think about someone you love with all your heart. Remember a time when you where blissfully happy and full of positive energy. Notice that your body is responding in kind to your thoughts. When you are frightened, stressed or overworked, the body reflects its physical version of your physiological and emotional realities.

Your thoughts and what you give your attention to do not exist in a vacuum. You are a hard-wired being. There is a direct and immediate relationship between what you think, how you feel and the way your body responds to all of the above. Your body eavesdrops in on your thinking; it is a feedback process. You are continually reacting, neurologically and chemically, to your thoughts and emotions. Making your mind your friend is about harmonizing the mind, body and emotions, because your mind is more than just the brain, the white and grey matter in the cranium. The mind is the sum total of all the forms of intelligence that make up the totality of the human experience: emotions, thoughts, perceptions, experiences and beliefs. If you value and desire vibrant and robust health, you will need your awareness to be a willing, co-creative partner in that journey.

As I have mentioned previously, the one eternal relationship, that one persistent, unyielding component in your life, is you. No matter where you go there you are. Self-knowledge starts with realizing that the inescapable, unchanging component to life is you… and how you relate to yourself and how you feel about yourself. The body, as a lifelong partner in our personal growth, has a very important role in the know thyself quest. The body does not have an ego or unconscious agenda. It is simply reflecting and responding to what you do with your attention. Anyone who has ever struggled with weight issues knows how the inner unresolved needs for comfort and to experience life as sweet, show up as additional physical pounds that are put on in a futile effort to eat away unhappiness or boredom. People suffering with high blood pressure or ulcers know all too well how the body takes the brunt of heated thoughts and emotions run rampant. The origin of these biological ailments begins with our internally chosen responses to external stimuli and situations that go unexamined, uncontrolled and unmanaged. Proof once again that the unexamined life is not worth living. Anytime you think you have dealt with a troubling issue, take a look at how your body is responding. After all, it does not lie or deceive, unlike the ego or elected political officials.

In the process of making your mind your friend and harmonizing your body/mind connection, there is a very simple but powerful habit you can practice. That is giving your attention to what you *do* want... and not to want you don't want. It may seem incredibly self-evident, however for most people their mental landscape is absolutely cluttered with an obsessive inner dialogue that focuses on lack, scarcity, bad-faith in oneself and a non-productive disparagement about everything from global political issues to "does this outfit make my butt look big?" Just watch all the stories your attention plays through over the time frame of a single day. How many times a day do you imagine bills you cannot pay? How many times do you envision others not finding you acceptable or worthy of love? How many times do you re-enforce, with your attention, that you will never be happy? Just to underscore this point ask yourself how many times do you think, "What else can go wrong?" Why not ask yourself, "What else can go right?" Different sides of the same coin, yes, but the real question is: every time you flip that coin does it always land on 'tails' and never land on 'heads'?

Most of us are laboring under the misguided notion that focusing on all the possible things that could go wrong or might blow up in our faces is the most effective hyper-vigilant strategy to ensure that all the things we do want, which by the way is getting precious little of our attention, will infallible come to us. It is like watering and feeding all the weeds in your garden yet expecting only the flowers and fruit bearing plants to bloom and grow.

Worrying is just another name for the well-practiced habit of empowering more of what you do *not* want to bring into your life. This self-sabogoting, re-enforced mindset is not natural. No child is born obsessed with giving their attention to worst possible scenerios. They are too busy playing and being present for what they do have. Remember when you were a child. When you played house or doctor, did you ever imagine that you would not be able to pay your bills and the bank would take back your home or business or you would get sued for malpractice? Did you ever imagine that the insurance rates were too high and one good flood would wipe you out? Of course not. You had to *learn* how to eclipse your present point of focus and assert potentially destructive things into your line of thought. You learned this inner behavior. You can now learn something else... something better.

Creating a new learning pattern for how to organize your mind begins with the little things. Start by releasing the grasp you have on the smaller things you faithfully imagine conspiring aganist you. Next time you get in a checkout lane at a store or change lanes on the highway, stop telling yourself, "Watch, now that I'm in this line it will become the slowest." Cease cultivating the story that money is scheming its way out your wallet and bank account everytime you pick up your checkbook or go to the mailbox and see a bill. Stop envisioning annoying, microbrained people going out of their way to ruin your day. Most events that find us in life are the perfect oppportunites for taking our peace of mind back. After all aren't these minor set backs exactly how we practiced giving our personal power away and tormenting ourselves in the first place?

When you practice on the more manageable, minute details, you will have the skill when you need it most for maintaining balance when the really big things come your way. No one on the planet Earth is immune to experiencing the whole of life: the good, the bad, the pleasant, the unsavory. Making your mind your friend is priceless should you ever find yourself dealing with a divorce, bankrupcy, sensitive legal issues, challenging medical diagonsis. Now is the time to gain mastery over what you willinging choose to invest in with your attention. There is a plethora of things in the world that legitimately do not have your best interest at heart... no reason to make your relationship with your mind one of them.

Play... The Ultimate Freedom

*E*ver consider that everyone is born knowing how to play? Imagine for a moment where the human race would be if we were born not knowing how to suckle? Life would be all too short. If we are all born with an instinctive knowledge for something, that wisdom must be pretty important to life itself.

Without play what would be the point of life? As Jack Nicholson so aptly put it in a Stephen King collaboration, "All work and no play makes Jack a dull boy;" not to mention unhappy and unhealthy. And from the looks of it, Jack has had no shortage of play. But play does more for us than entertain an otherwise dreary existence. Play liberates the mind, the emotions, the very soul of our being.

Consider all the money you spend on "stuff" in an attempt to buy some sense of emotional satisfaction. No matter how much you purchase, your life would still be unfulfilling without play? What good is that big flat screen television if all you watch is the crisis news network, CNN? How much use is that party dress without the party? You can drop tons of cash, max out your credit cards and still never get the value you do from play.

That's the best part about play... IT'S FREE! It does not mat-

21

ter what your credit report looks like, no one can repossess your ability to derive joy from life. On the flip side, you can have a fat bank account, but if you have no fun in your life, are you really rich? What inner wealth do you have if you can't even amuse yourself? All play requires is your imagination which is unlimited and boundless. Set that inner child free from the adult prison it has been locked in, serving a life sentence. Consider it kind of like parole. Only make it a play release program instead of work release.

Play is free from regulation; no government mandates or paper-work required. Call it your 401 Play plan. It's an investment in you. You are free to make contributions at any time and you do not have to be retired to enjoy the benefits. The only modifica-tions necessary to your current plan involve the elimination of that serious and uptight attitude. You have to be willing to put down your attachment to worry and unhappiness. I suspect that is the price of admission most people feel they can afford with-out too much sacrifice.

Without play how would we learn to grow? Wait a minute… learning without fun, forced growth, boredom… that was my last business meeting and seminar schedule. Development minus the playful element leaves us with rigid, authoritarian, threatening and burdened methods of self-extension. Hardly seems worth coming to the planet for. Perhaps a play-deprived existence costs us more than we bargained for.

Eastern philosophies define enlightenment as being in the present moment and not having a problem with it. Consider that enlightenment is the ultimate in across the board states of freedom, liberation from constraint and limitation… hmm that sounds like play to me. You simply cannot get freer than en-lightenment. Now reflect back to when you were a kid playing house. Did it ever occur to you to add to the imaginary scenario that you had too many bills to pay or not enough hours in the day? When you played doctor, did you determine if the patient had health insurance or could even pay your bill? Of course not. Hey, the fact is you were practicing medicine without a license! Didn't think about that, did you? But if you did give those types of things your attention, you would cease to play. You would no longer be in the present moment and not have a problem with it. When we play, these states of limitation never even enter our thoughts. That is the power and beauty of play.

Some say you can meditate your way to enlightenment. Others say it can be done with a vow of poverty or silence. Personally if I have any choice in the matter, and we all in fact do have free will, I would choose to play my way into a fully liberated state of existence. The enlightened ones are not necessarily on a mountaintop in Tibet; they could be the ones in the sandbox at the playground.

5 Tips For A More Playful You:

- **Get out of your head** ~ Play is a heart centered, heart driven reality. Play expands your perspective far beyond the limits of the frontal lobe. Trust in that free fall from the head into the heart. It is safe, it is healing and it is enjoyable.

- **Play is how you liberate your inner child** ~ Ever wonder where your sense of wonder and adven-ture went? It is in mothballs with your inner child.

The inner child does not have to do the dishes or get the kids to school on time. However the inner child does make playing in the soap and water fun while you're getting those dishes washed. The inner child also knows how to sing and connect with your kids while driving them to school. Wouldn't that turn a chore into joy?

- **Play is how you laugh at yourself** ~ When you can laugh at life's flaws and mishaps it always takes that stinging pain out of taking life so tragically personal and turns it into a healing. Laughing at your best efforts gone awry provides you the necessary psychological distance needed for shaking off disappointment and moving forward.

- **Play does not belong on a calendar, it belongs in the flow of life** ~ If you isolate play until the schedule allows, you will find that something "more important" will always eclipse that play date. On your deathbed will you regret that you played more and worked less? Don't wait until it is too late. Open your mind now and let in the playfulness.

- **Play is regenerating** ~ Play is how we restore the inner juiciness and vitality of life. Play is how the body and mind relax so that there is not such a constant outflow of "busy" energy depleting the human experience. If meditation is just not your thing, rejuvenate and replenish by playing with your dog or cat. They are the ultimate play gurus.

The "N" Word

Whatever happened to our immunity to verbal weaponry? In our youth, armed with the mantra, "sticks and stones may break my bones, but words will never hurt me," off we went into the real world. But we soon returned shaken and crying when someone called us a name.

Maybe the real problem is we never actually believed we possessed that enlightened linguistic state of Teflon-like strength. Personally, I have a more Buddhist stance on this issue: words are inherently neutral. Words have no special sovereignty over humans. The sole basis for this power to exalt or devastate is the authority we project upon them. We give words the power to insult, the power to injure and only we can end that tyranny and take our power back.

Very few people have answered this call. Lenny Bruce and more recently Russell Brand mastered freedom over the articulated arsenal. When Brand appeared on Jimmy Fallon's late night talk show (3-11-09), Jimmy expressed a mild emotional/psychological convulsion (I call it a vapor lock) over something Brand had just shared. Russell Brand, completely at ease, gently repeated over and over again, as if administering a vocalized homeopathic remedy, "Jimmy, they are only words; they are only words." Thank you Russell Brand. Finally! Someone who is willing to stand up and publicly point out the obvious: words are abstract ideas that take on the form and shape *you* give them. No one jumps into your mind and poisons your response. You alone are accountable for their interpretation by what you choose with your free will.

Recently I had my own up close and personal opportunity to join the Bruce and Brand "words will never hurt me" line dance. My manager had scheduled a radio interview, something I do quite frequently. It started out in the usual way. The producer called at the designated time and asked me to hold for the host. From the start it was not a normal interview.

The first thing that struck me as odd was the host was very difficult to understand. Most radio professionals speak lucidly and articulate well; not so with this man. I was challenged to clearly understand exactly what he was saying. The interview starts with a few questions about some unusual products on my website. This is followed by another perfectly reasonable question. As I start to answer, he interrupts me. I have no clue what he is asking me, as it all sounds like one garbled mess. I ask him to repeat himself. He does. I still have no idea what the radio host is saying. I ask him to repeat himself again. He does; I am still completely lost. I am also rather embarrassed to keep asking him to repeat the question, so I decide to answer the original question he asked before the interruption.

The radio show host stops me again to ask another question. Okay, I get it now! This guy is a shock jock, and he has been baiting me with lewd suggestions about the use of these products. My first impulse is to simply hang up and get on with my busy day. Then I thought, "No, this guy thinks he has some ordinary person on the line who believes that words have the ability to oppress. Clearly he has gone to my website, seen that I am a spiritual teacher, and figured if he could rattle my cage, I would blurt out a few highly charged sound bites he could replay for his own entertainment. I don't think so. Instead, I'm going to have some fun with this guy." He may have been to my website, but he clearly hasn't read any of my books or articles, especially those on the power of words.

When he finally figured out he could not upset my cool and calm demeanor with his obscene rantings, he moved on to Plan "B." He started tossing out the "F" bombs. When he stops, I reply with, "Well sir, that is one of the most enjoyable and pleasurable activities two loving people can engage in, and I want to thank you for wishing me such a richly successful experience of intimate happiness. And may I take this opportunity to wish you the same."

Now the guy is really stuttering. He is losing ground fast. This is not a good situation if you are a shock jock. He has completely lost control of the interview and is grasping for anything he can verbally sling my way to upset the balance of power. As it happens in the most desperate of conversational circumstances, he calls me the dreaded "C" word. Too bad he could not see the beatific smile it brought to my face. I simply chuckled and said, "As you well know, that is a very important part of the female anatomy, and I am delighted to be one."

By this time he was in professional agony, twisting wildly in the wind of my unfettered feedback. I, on the other hand, had grown pretty bored with the whole process. I thought, "If this is the very best this man can do, I'm done. The evolved thing to do would be to take him out of his own self-created misery." So I thanked him for his time, sexual blessings and female anatomical acknowledgement, and with that I hung up the phone.

My business partner was in the room at the time. Hearing only my side of the conversation, he was all smiles, having figured out shortly into the game what was going on. "I suspect that he won't be calling back, and your interview will never see the light of day. It never looks good for the guest to shock the shock jock." I nodded in agreement and had a vision of the poor man, head buried in his hands crying, "But boss, I tried! I just couldn't insult the woman no matter what I did." And the show's producer attempting to comfort the unraveled host with inspirational words, "Don't worry buddy, I'm sure you will traumatize the next spiritual teacher we have on. Everything's going to be okay."

Words can only harm you if you capitulate to the assault. You existed before other people with bad manners and questionable choices of words, and you will exist after. Everyone has free will, and we are fortunate to live in a country that protects free speech. This means you will never be able to control what other people say or when they say it. Instead of vainly attempting to constrain what other people can or cannot say, doesn't it simply make more sense to free *your* mind instead? If the same phrase were spoken in a language you did not understand, would it still bother you?

So precisely what is the "N" word? The "N" word is Neutrality. All words are the "N" word; all words *are* neutral. I suspect that was not the neutral "N" word response you were expecting. Furthermore, I suspect it would benefit us all if we would now take the time to realize our fondest childhood wish and finally declare with conviction, "Words will never hurt me."

Are You Possessed?

*I*was talking with a loved one who rode out Hurricane Ike on Galveston Island on the gulf coast of Texas. The Island took a big hit with a 14-foot storm surge, 120mph winds and torrential rain. As will happen in the aftermath of a storm of this magnitude, a significant amount of the residents' possessions were destroyed. Large piles of rubbish, that only days before had been coveted items of ownership, were now stacked into curbside shrines to the awesome power of Mother Nature - or more appropriately, monuments to our insatiable appetite for mindless consumer spending.

Household items were scattered everywhere, removed from houses in their owners' futile attempt to salvage what they could by drying out what the mold and humidity had not yet claimed. My loved one remarked in amazement at the sheer quantity of "stuff" everyone owned. It seemed unimaginable that people could squeeze so many "things" into their living spaces, once you saw the entire inventory on display. Where did it all go? Every-one on his block had a treadmill! Most looked brand new. (If you could see the neighbors, most probably were.) Everyone was armed and had spray-painted signs on fences that warned of the dangers of thinking this was a self-service yard sale. Pos-sessions are possessions, even if they are worthless. One of the

33

State Troopers, leading two looters into the back of his car, was overheard quoting Thoreau, "Most of the luxuries and many of the so-called comforts of life are not only *not* indispensable, but positive hindrances to the elevation of mankind." I don't think they got it.

But it is not just disasters that bring this clutter loving consciousness to the surface. How many times have you moved and asked yourself, "Where did I get all this crap?" In some insidious manner these physical objects gradually take over of our lives. Do we own our possessions or do they own us?

My first summer between college years, I moved to a beach community. There was a man there I encountered frequently who I thought was homeless. I'd see him on bus benches always wearing the same clothes. Leaves stuck in his hair gave him the appearance that he had just awakened from sleeping on the ground in a park. Sometimes I would see him wandering around town. He seemed to walk for miles everyday. Clearly he had no job. One of the locals branded him a casualty of the 60's who took too much LSD and never came down. His brother, who lived in town, took care of him, making sure he had food and clothes.

One morning as I was running along the beach, I saw this semi-homeless man. He had dug a large hole that cut him off at the knees when he stood in it. The locals had assured me that the man was harmless, and there was no need to be afraid of him. As I ran up and down the beach I noticed he had a long stick, and he was drawing something in the sand. Curiosity got the best of me. On my last lap, I decided to stop by and see what he was so busy creating. Upon approaching I introduced myself. The man looked up and smiled warmly. He had been absorbed in the task of drawing stick figures with the greatest of concentration. I did not wish to appear rude, so I pointed at one of the stick figures and complimented him on how realistic his drawing looked. The man proudly smiled and informed me this was a portrait of his brother. Then the smile slowly faded and the man shook his head sadly and said, "It's too bad about my brother." "What happened to him?" I inquired gently. "He has a house," came the simple answer. "He has a house?" I repeated, not sure I was following the line of tragedy. "Yes," the man replied thoughtfully. "My brother and I used to do things together and go places. Then he got a house, and now the house needs him to do things. He does not do things with me anymore because he has to do things for the house, and he cannot go anywhere with me because the house has him." The man continued to shake his head sadly. "I will not go into houses," he said with resolve. "I will go to my brother's house, but I will not go inside. Because once you go inside... that's it... the house *has you!* It will always need something, and that's how 'it' gets you."

I never had the opportunity to talk with the beach artist again, but nearly thirty years later, I still cannot forget our conversation. Through what many might label a distorted perspective, this man conveyed a clear message with gravity and insight. I have reflected back many times on that brief encounter on the beach and wondered where I was allowing the possessions in my life to own me.

It has occurred to me over the years how interesting and revealing our use of the word "possessions" is. How many of us allow our lives to be possessed by our homes, cars or boats? God knows the women from *Sex In The City* were clearly possessed by their shoe collections. But this is a human issue, not a gender issue. I have seen men possessed by everything from their baseball card collections, to their garages full of tools, to the love of their life - their car.

Over a hundred years ago Henry David Thoreau, the noted transcendentalist philosopher, wrote, "A man is rich in proportion to the number of things he can afford to let alone." In his writings he warned of the dangers of inheriting even the fewest and simplest of objects as a way of opening oneself up to the type of possession we are discussing here, as another way of waking up one day to discover your life is overrun and polluted with the accumulation of "things". Thoreau did not define poverty consciousness the way most of us do today when he wrote, "However mean your life is, meet it and live it; do not shun it and call it hard names. Cultivate poverty like a garden herb, like sage. Do not trouble yourself much to get new things, whether clothes or friends. Things do not change, we change. Sell your clothes and keep your thoughts."

Consider that this warning came long before our ability to microchip our entire music collection on a single iPod or our entire business on a laptop. Our ability to condense our valuables into smaller and smaller spaces has only fueled our prowess and vulnerability to becoming increasing more possessed by our possessions. High-tech possession for a high-tech world.

Perhaps there is a blessing within these life-riddled catastrophes such as floods, relocations and fires that force an involuntary purging of possessions. Thoreau offers words of wisdom for those who may find themselves unwillingly separated from a lifetime of property they have worked hard to amass: "As you simplify your life, the laws of the universe will be simpler; solitude will not be solitude, poverty will not be poverty, nor weakness weakness."

Another unexpected gift of finding oneself materialistically stripped naked is the opportunity to reevaluate what is truly important and really valuable to us. To consciously update what we want to surround ourselves with and to reconsider what is authentically worth our investment. As the great Oscar Wilde once said, "We know the price of everything and the value of nothing."

For those readers who may be piecing their lives back together after an unexpected loss, may I leave you with one more priceless non-material gift from Thoreau: "There is no value in life except what you choose to place upon it and no happiness in any place except what you bring to it yourself"... and to my semi-homeless beach buddy out there, wherever you are, may you continue to be as free as the day you were born.

Cultural Poison to the West - Panacea to the East

*W*hen the Eastern systems of self-healing examine health and balance, they offer a very different paradigm than our more familiar "Western" point of view. The differences are most noticeable and significant when it comes to understanding the nature of the individual life and the life of the collective. For example, from the Eastern perspective, there will never be one single pill, diet, exercise or lifestyle that will cure what ails *all* people. Every person is a microcosmic Universe unto themselves. Each person is unique and must be understood, examined and healed separately from the rest of humanity.

This philosophy is not just limited to the comprehensive understanding of an individual's physical well being. It applies to every aspect of a person's life. What is experientially, emotionally and perceptually toxic to one person could be liberating to another. There is not one accepted standard that will equally measure every nuance of every person's life. The "average person" does not exist in Eastern philosophy. Each person, each case, is unique… a completely separate reality unto itself.

So it is when it comes to career development and the turmoil in our present job market. The media has dominated the intellectual landscape with reports of dire changes, catastrophic employment shifts and unsustainable economic losses. "How will I ever find a job when millions of people are out of work? My world situation is dire, catastrophic and unsustainable. Hey, where have I heard that before?" Just because CNN is selling across the board economic fear doesn't mean you have to buy it. You have free will. And, that may not be *your* Universe.

While the need to live within one's means is not disputed, what is debilitating in one person's reality may actually be liberating and powerfully transformative in another's. Shaking up the status quo is an opportunity to make different choices, to take another career path. Just because Fox News tells you everyone is losing their jobs does not mean you have the whole story. Human evolution allows old, tired and outdated methods of expansion to die out. If life has offered you a new set of circumstances, it is Nature's way of saying, "You are ready to grow in a new direction; there is nothing left for you in the old way; move on." Focus on breakthrough by taking and making the most of this fortuitous event rather than being paralyzed by breakdown from lamenting the loss of what you have grown beyond.

Your neighbors lost their jobs and are in crisis. Does that mean there is a career crisis in your world? You are a Universe unto yourself. That employment setback may be your neighbors' next biggest opportunity to re-evaluate their lives and what is important to them. It does not mean you need to bookmark Monster. com or other online headhunters, or spend sleepless nights worrying about your job security. There is not one developmental-driving reality that visits all people simultaneously.

Crisis, dire, catastrophic, impossible are all different names for fear. From a bigger picture perspective, what is presently occurring is a global fear epidemic spreading locally. Not by germ or bacteria but rather by worldview. The outer world conditions again reflect the inner world conditions. What that means is just because some people get the flu, doesn't mean everyone on the planet is sick or even going to get sick. When you refuse to accept change when it appears in your microcosmic Universe, you have not only opened the door to suffering, but also personally invited it in, offered it drinks and a comfortable place to stay.

The details of life on Earth will always be changing; that is the nature of this impermanent world. Nothing here stays for long. Everything on the planet has a shelf life. What were the only consistent career choices a hundred years ago versus today's world, aside from undertaking, tax collecting and prostitution? There are none. The job you thought was a safe and secure employment two years ago may not even exist today. Even the pace of change has gained speed and momentum. The more we as a global community advance, the faster these changes will take place.

Eastern Spiritual philosophies point out the shortcomings to an inherent basic human desire: control. We attempt to control every detail of the outer world and hold it in a fixed place, until we have everything right where we want it to be. We all desire to create a comfortable external reality and then maintain that position forever. We want to solve a problem once in our lives and then never have to revisit it again. We want to find a job once then never have to deal with job or career transitions again. We invest in a position of some kind and expect it to pay us dividends the rest of our lives. What this leads to is an escalated experience of personal suffering due to the inescapable reality that life is constantly in a state of flux, change and motion, forever vulnerable and subject to the permeable forces of life on Earth.

You are no different than your 401K! Just as the macrocosmic Universe is ever-growing, expanding and changing, so it is with your microcosmic Universe. Things will orbit, eclipse and even from time to time collide with your world. That is what it means to be human and a Universe unto yourself.

At our finest, we are designed to be flexible, resilient, open to change and sensitive to growth potential. The paradox of the human experience is that we are built for rapid and sudden adaptation, but we *want* everything perfectly organized and in its place, and we want it to all stay that way or else! Just because we are created to go with the mutable flow does not make us immune to primitive responses such as rigidity, fearfulness, inflexibility and unreasonable stubbornness. Just because we have achieved a specific quality of livelihood doesn't mean there will not be an opportunity to upgrade and evolve to the next level. Just because some people are screaming the sky is falling doesn't mean your name is "Chicken Little." The Western concept that there is only one reality, and that it is a ubiquitous truth is merely an illusion.

Technology and how we relate to reality is changing so rapidly, how could we possibly imagine that job descriptions and positions would not change at the same rate to accommodate these new, more effective variations? When job loss is at an all time high, it is an invitation to reinvent ourselves, our skills and talents, and to dare to explore the dreams and potentials that have lived outside of our previous comfort zone, our occupationally-challenged box. Imagine what the world would be like if computers were suppressed because they were going to displace millions of people's jobs. Steve Jobs of Apple wouldn't have had a job or a company. I guess that would make him just Steve or Steve Jobless.

For every loss, we, as unlimited Spiritual beings, have both the power and potential to invent a new wheel, create another source of fire, mine previously unexplored inner forms of gold. After all, this planet was constructed so that we could realize and unfold the evolution of our souls. While living in an environment that was manifested solely for the purpose of our awakening to the reality of our unlimited true nature, words like loss, failure, useless and unwanted really need to be redefined. What also require redefining are ideas like success, valuable and a willingness to experience the present moment as an opportunity to move forward.

Here are some alternative definitions:

> "Success is not a place at which one arrives but rather the spirit with which one undertakes and continues the journey." ~ Author Unknown.

> "Success is the ability to go from one failure to another with no loss of enthusiasm." ~ Winston Churchill

We have come here to learn and grow. Should we discover along the way that what we have been doing is no longer working for us, that we must find a more life enhancing way to relate to our problems and life challenges, then we have not failed. We have matured. We have found ourselves in a position where we must require more from ourselves and demand greater accountability from those who have applied for the jobs of public servants. If you do not like the direction things are taking, do not behave like a child or let people get away with irresponsible, greedy behavior. You are not powerless or a victim... unless you want that in your Universe.

Nations and global communities have always benefited from a population that was open to learning a better way to respond to outdated ways of relating to the infrastructure of life. If this were not true there would be no civil rights movement, the wall in Berlin would still be standing, there would be no United Nations, there would still be a US embargo against Cuba.... uh, what? There still is? Ok, forget that last one.

Don't let fear control and dictate the limits of your life. When life presents an opportunity disguised as a set back, reach around the illusion and seize the day. And if you are one of the people sitting back waiting on the government for assistance, I offer you what Groucho Marx would tell you: "Politics is the art of looking for trouble, finding it everywhere, diagnosing it incorrectly and applying the wrong remedies." I think that could qualify as a Divine Law. I know it already is one in Washington.

Bumper Sticker Wisdom

*E*ver notice how so many of the bumper sticker messages out there are simple yet profound? I saw a great one recently that said **Life is the Classroom. Love is the Lesson**. That pretty much says it all. How is it that all the great spiritual sayings can fit on a bumper sticker? The reason is that Universal truth is simple and straightforward. To mention a few: **Be Here Now,** and **You Are What You Love and You Love Whatever You Give Your Attention To**, and **You Do Not Have Love, You *ARE* Love**. My all-time favorite is **The Truth Shall Set You Free**. Anytime I'm looking at a spiritual point of view that is pedantically over complicated, I know the essence of the truth has gotten lost in the shuffle.

Please: Do Not Feed the Ego.

The purpose of all created life is to learn and grow. That is every sentient being's job description. Whatever lesson you sign up for depends on what you give your attention to. The great 18th century scientist/mystic, Emanuel Swedenborg (1682-1772), voted by Stanford University to be one of the wisest people to have ever lived on the planet, wrote a great deal about this very subject matter. If I were to simplify his volumes of wisdom into a bumper sticker, it would be: **You *are* Consciousness; it is Not a Possession**. You do not have it; you are it. Consciousness is love.

You do not have to spend your life trying to earn love. Life has never been about working to be deserving and worthy enough. How do you prove that you are worthy enough of something that you already are? Life is all about learning you are love and embracing this truth. It is about recognizing you are love and no one and no thing has the power to change that.

Who Put a Stop Payment on my Reality Check?

Swedenborg describes the human experience as coming with a built-in, self-corrective guidance system. It is better known as the nervous system; what I like to call the "keep it real arena." When you give your attention to seeing yourself as something more limited than love, you feel it immediately. There is no confusion here in the planet Earth classroom. When you see yourself as the person who does not have enough money, time or opportunity, you feel that limitation right away. When you give your attention to seeing yourself as connected to the source of all abundance and wellbeing, you feel that expansiveness as well. Your body, via the nervous system, lets you know in no uncertain terms if you are choosing to learn from a limited classroom or an unlimited classroom, depending of course, on what you give your attention to. **Life is a Journey. Enjoy the Ride or Die Trying.**

Change is Inevitable...
Except from a Vending Machine.

Anytime I pick up a book and the author is telling me I have to ask myself ten or more different questions in response to every life situation or relationship, I immediately become apprehensive. It wouldn't fit on a bumper sticker. Or if I sign up for a self-improvement class and the curriculum involves taking a string of other classes in order to achieve clarity, my gut feeling is to walk away immediately. Learning about yourself is easier and more direct than successfully performing a never-ending series of stupid human tricks. You come direct from the manufacturer equipped with everything you need to know about what you are, why you are here and what you are choosing to learn from.

The More You Complain, the Longer God Makes You Live

Pay attention to how what you give your attention to makes you feel. As one sticker states, **Pain is inevitable, Misery is optional.** Is the inner narrative you are loyally focusing on making your life feel hellishly limited? Stop. You have free will. You can choose something else. The tricky part is how much of your life is run on autopilot? How much of what you give your attention to is grossly repetitive and not consciously examined and updated? Are you repeatedly self-inflicting some critical or harsh words someone else put into motion? Do you still see yourself through the filter of a parent's or teacher's opinion that defines you as incapable of doing anything right? Do you constantly tell yourself you are ugly and unlovable because this idea was solidified when you were a teenager or going through an awkward stage of development? The purpose of life is to grow beyond anything that separates you from the truth about your identity as love. And let's face it, life offers us many creative and "up close and personal" opportunities to do just that.

So here are the most important points I learned from reading bumper stickers.

- **You *are* love** – I can't add anything to that.

- **Love: it's your spiritual identity** - and it is experienced as consciousness, as awareness.

- **What we think we become** - When you give something your attention, you are giving it your love, because you are not separate from love.

- **You are what you love & you love whatever you give your attention to** - my favorite

- **Who feels it knows it** - When you give attention to limited things, you feel limited, unlike when you focus on the unlimited. How does it make you feel?

- **A day without sunshine is like night** - If what you are giving your attention to is not setting you free, you have not seen the truth yet; keep looking.

All this easy to master and understand wisdom can fit on a subcompact. How good is that! Maybe this is why bumper sticker philosophy compels us to speed up and get close enough to read it... because the truth is oftentimes simply stated and right in front of us. So the next time you are stuck in traffic, use it as a learning experience and start checking out the wisdom on the cars around you. Happy motoring!

If I'm Not At Square One, I'll Be Back Shortly

I have had to start over so many times in so many aspects of my life, you'd think Square One was my mailing address. I'm sure we at least share the same zip code. I have been diagnosed terminal twice. Yes, twice. I like to refer to myself as a "terminal" over achiever. Back to Square One. I have been lied to and cheated on by nearly every single romantic partner I have ever had. For me that is a deal breaker. The instant I discovered the betrayal, I packed up and left… destination? Square One. Once again I found myself engaged in the never-ending process of reviving and repairing my life. Due to chronic health problems I lost my business which I spent nearly a decade building. It took every cent I had ever saved just trying to stay alive. I had to start over financially from Square One. I have been without a home, and as Blanch DuBois from "Streetcar Named Desire" would say, "…have relied on the kindness of strangers." No home? No problem. I can stay at Square One… they'll even leave the light on for ya. There is nothing about life deconstruction and self-resurrection I fail to understand. After all, practice does make perfect. By now I should be as perfect and flawless as a diamond.

The best thing about mastering the profound understanding of how to start over ubiquitously is that when something comes to an end in my life, and let's face it in this world things come and go like confetti in the wind, I now waste no time in accepting it, and getting down to the business of growing beyond whatever no longer serves me or has fallen away.

What I have found is that starting over is just another name for growth… unobstructed, unlimited growth. And I ask you, what is life without growth? When I think about it, growth itself really isn't that scary. As a baby I certainly had no issues with it. As a matter of fact, as an infant that was my full-time job. As a teenager, I couldn't wait to grow into an adult. Without growth I would never have recovered from illness, trauma, heartbreak or the vaporization of cash from the black hole formerly known as my 401K.

Starting over has taught me how to trust in myself. Life renovations consistently invite me to raise the bar on reclaiming my value, power and worth. Every time life seems to strip me down to my "naked truth," I know I have the ability, the intelligence and the sheer raw nerve to put my life back together. The fear of having to start over has lost its power to paralyze. At this point, I have far too much real life experience to draw upon to be daunted by that retro threat. I have hard-earned immunity. I am no longer intimidated by the prospect of finding myself once again enrolled in the Life 101 classroom, taught at the Square One campus. I have witnessed the person of substance within me work through any setback and just keep moving forward. I now feel comforted by past lessons of loss. They have ingrained a living relationship of trust, in myself and my abilities, that no one and no thing can take from me. I now know how to believe in and value my own strengthens. I have developed the faith and discipline to focus on what is within me rather than what has changed outside of me. Every time life takes something away, another precious nugget of self-awareness and self-knowledge has been gained and deepened.

With every rebuilding circumstance, my return engagement to Square One is an opportunity to reinvent who I am and how I experience myself. What outgrown story, outdated role or mold will I destroy next? Inherent in every new beginning is an empowered occasion to eliminate bad habits or unhealthy behaviors that are not improving the quality of my life. It is so easy when things do not change or get shaken up to remain loyal or unconsciously committed to things that are not life-enhancing. When everything falls apart, the gift is the conscious and deliberate re-piecing of only the best and most useful of what I know. Starting over grants me permission to actively edit my lifestyle, inner dialogue and delete whatever I do not wish to take with me into my new life.

I have observed with great delight and entertainment that starting over and being stuck in a rut never co-exist. Square One is where I can always trade in my old, rundown stuck existence for a new high-performance life. Every time I practice refurbishing any area of my life, I am really actualizing the creation of an upgraded version of myself. I am tapping into the option to expand my self-definition. As I let go of every old habit, useless or self-destructive pattern or limited way of relating to myself, I am refining and extending the reach of my personal growth. Any time the flow of life gives me the opportunity to exchange "stagnation" for "enlivened" it is a blessed opportunity to me.

Culturally speaking, I have found that starting over at Square One has a bad reputation. Collectively we seek to avoid it, smearing it with excuses like: "I have worked all this time for nothing; now I have to leave everything useful and meaningful behind me; nothing else in my life will ever work." This "crash and burn" means once again I'm playing "Survivor" on the Square One reality series, but what I have joyously discovered is that within every new beginning are the glorious and highly potent seeds of excitement. Like any other seeds, these do not just spring up and yield something tangible without the proper environment. These seeds have to be watered with the truth that I am a wiser person now from what I have learned, and I can move forward fearlessly with greater accumulated experiential knowledge. These seeds need to be nurtured with patience, which happens when I take the time to collect myself, so that I move forward as a whole person and not as a fragmented, injured victim.

The seeds also need to find good soil in which to grow. Soil that is properly tilled and maintained, which occurs naturally every time I rein in my attention and focus on the positive, what I *do* want, and not on the negative, what I don't want to happen. These excitement seeds have the space to flourish when I habitually weed out all the thoughts that do not support the new direction I am choosing, and I cease looking backwards, because I'm simply too committed to looking forward. When I create a new response to life challenges and setbacks, anything is possible. That is a quality of excitement that comes with a much longer shelf life than anything purchased on a "therapeutic" shopping spree.

I have learned that embedded within every setback is the prized opportunity to evolve to a higher level. I know I have thought many times, "If only I had a do-over!" Then I realize I do have a do-over. It's called Square One... starting over, new beginnings, growing beyond what has hurt or limited me. Only now I have my inner consciousness primed and ready for a brand new accelerated experience of expansion. I have learned from past pains when to trust my instincts when something is wrong, even if I cannot quite put my finger on exactly what is amiss. I have come to value that without starting over at Square One, I would have to use an old, somewhat shaky foundation to build something original. I would have to use the same piece of paper every time I wanted to write something new. Worse than that, I would have to wear the same fashion outfit everyday. A heinous crime that makes every woman shudder at the mere thought of; not to mention I'd end up on the Most Wanted list of the Fashion Police. But then I diverge.

I have seen that failure, disappointment, oppression and breakdowns are the launching pads to self-correction and self-realization. Suffering is how I self-correct. Without it how would I know when I was off course? Every time I bounce back my faith in myself blooms and thrives. Life has taught me that resilience is an emotional, psychological and spiritual muscle: use it or lose it. Resiliency allows me to access and draw on a greater brilliance and inner intelligence that I need when creating a new beginning. Flexibility is how I grow beyond fear and insecurity. I am now aware that every time life throws me something unexpected, and I have to resuscitate some dimension of my existence, I can draw on a vigorous quality of self-reliance and a depth of self-confidence in my ability to abundantly renew.

Every time I have been in the midst of a life-altering event I have noticed a tendency to become myopic in scope. It would be only in hindsight that I managed a self-reflective perception that aligned me with the truth that these situations, tragic at the time, propelled me into an enhanced version of life. I look back on my romantic relationships that broke up like the Titanic, and thank those men for their cheating ways. After all it was that action, in the end, that liberated me from the burden of those deceptive, fraudulent and misguided relationships. I am grateful for the very first time I was diagnosed terminal. It forced me to revamp my lifestyle and establish infinitely healthier eating, exercise and life management choices. It also gave me time to build a strong foundation of knowledge from which I constructed my recovery program when I was injured in a life threatening car accident years later.

I have grown into the realization that the path of life is not always straight and narrow. Oftentimes the road we find ourselves standing on has many unexpected twists and turns. Releasing resistance to beginning anew is how I now know to zig, when I was zagging. It is how I feel my way through life's many blind curves. It is how I see and know which fork in the road to take. And yes, sometimes it seems like all roads lead to Square One. I just remember that life is a journey, covering lots of territory, and there is no wisdom in letting the bumps in the road determine how much ground I'm going to cover in my lifetime.

The best advice I could give when starting over is to get out of the head. The ego is not always my best friend. I will not listen to the ego run an inner narrative that is restrictive, negative or limited. The ego likes to tell me that I did not do something right or that I am not good enough. This is not the self-corrective intelligence to rely on when considering moving forward. My heart and my gut always know when I am being true to myself; the ego hasn't a clue. If the ego knew the all answers, I most likely would not have found myself in a position of having to start over to begin with. A genesis strategy always emerges organically when I embrace a loving, accepting, forgiving and patient relationship with myself. That is a quality of self-integration the head knows nothing about. The ego is purely a divide and conquer tyrannical dictator. The heart knows how to mend and heal; the gut knows what is true and right. Whenever I find myself back at Square One looking for new direction, I take the G.P.S. away from the ego, drop down into my heart, regroup and remind myself I am here on the planet to grow and learn, and life will never permit me to play hooky, so let's get going. The bottom line is that in the board game of life, Square One is more valuable real estate than Boardwalk and Park Place combined.

Me, Myself & Eye
True Confessions of a Cyclops

I was born with a very large cataract in the left eye and a syndrome that only occurs in female children. It caused the left eye to turn inward and to the right. The left eye would pull toward the nose in such an exaggerated manner that the pupil and iris could not be seen, leaving me with a quite decidedly one-eyed look.

My family never made fun of me. They never commented on the birth defect affecting my left eye. So when I started kindergarten, my first introduction into the "outside world," I was surprised and woefully unprepared. I was completely taken aback when the other children would look at me, scream and run away. I had no idea my schoolmates would respond so violently to a condition I only thought about when I had to go for an eye examination.

My parents had taken me in for cosmetic surgery several times since I was an infant in an attempt to correct the problem. Although the surgeries went well, the doctors fully expected that I would require another round of corrective surgical procedures by the time I hit puberty. The doctors had done the best they could but the correction would not be complete until my body stopped developing and muscle growth had stabilized. The bottom line was that I was stuck with this defect until my early twenties. My social life was swirling down the drain and I didn't even know it.

At the tender age of five, I had no concept that my face looked dramatically different from others even with the one eye turned grossly inwards. I did not know how to respond to the other children's reactions of calling me a "monster" and "cyclops." As I progressed through school, to say that things didn't get any better would be an understatement. In my elementary years I remember running home after school as fast as I could to outrun the other kids who were throwing rocks at me yelling, "Kill the freak, kill the freak!"

One day, after a particularly challenging stoning episode, I stood and stared at my face in the mirror. I just could not understand it. As far as I was concerned I still looked the same as I did *before* I became "the monster" to these other children. I just could not wrap my mind around what the other children found so horrible about my eye. Why did it seem to make me subhuman from their perspective?

In the small town where I grew up, as with all small towns, once you are given a label, it is yours to cherish for a lifetime or at least for what seemed that long. My nickname all through middle school and high school was "cyclops." Although the situation was gradually correcting itself as I got older, it was still highly visible. Visible enough that it was the first thing people noticed when they looked at me. I remember once in junior high school running and hiding in a stranger's garage to get away from two boys who were chasing me, determined to gouge out the offensive eye with a sharp stick. Looking different was not only socially detrimental but also a genuine threat to my physical wellbeing!

It was not until I went off to college that I was finally free of the town "freak" stigma. Even today, if you know what to look for, you can still see remnants of the irregular left eye movement. It had taken me nearly twenty years but now it was no longer an issue that poisoned every relationship I attempted to cultivate. At last I was gaining some distance from the emphasis on being "defective" and I was starting to appreciate the level and quality of self-development and self-acceptance this one-eyed look imposed upon my life.

I was a very private child. I spent a great deal of time playing by myself and developed a very healthy and strong sense of independence. I learned to value, respect and honor my relationship with myself. I focused on hobbies that cultivated and fostered my creativity. I was comfortable within my own skin and with my own companionship. I *knew* who I was, even if every last person on the planet wanted to stone me for being a freak. I knew I was a good, loving and very intelligent person. I was okay with myself, even if no one around me could validate or embrace that level of open, honest acceptance.

My appreciation for this unusual character building birth defect hit an inadvertent epiphany one evening. The actor William Windom was performing a one-man play of James Thurber writings. I paid an additional sum of money to attend an event after the performance where people could meet the actor and ask him questions. I recall there being a long line. I patiently waited my turn to speak with Mr. Windom, when a tall very attractive blonde woman stepped right in front of me as if I was not there and asked if Windom had any opinion as to why James Thurber was such a brilliant writer. Once again I felt eclipsed by the pretty girl that everyone wanted to talk to and befriend.

What William Windom uttered next both shocked and healed me. "Thurber was such a creative writer because he was born blind in one eye. He was a freak and his childhood was so painful he developed himself and his imagination in a way most people are never forced to," Windom explained. Confirmation at last! Yes, *this* has provided me with an inner strengthening and self-knowing…I knew it! "Are all people who are born blind in one eye 'freaks'?" I asked Windom, elbowing my way around the rude, buxom blonde. "Do you know any who are not?" He answered. "No," I thought to myself, "I don't." "I was born blind in one eye," I stammered aloud. Windom turned beet red and was clearly embarrassed to have said something he felt I might have taken as offensive. Of course this poor man had no way of knowing he was talking to the only "born blind in one eye" person within a ten thousand mile radius. And strangely enough, I felt deeply comforted. Validated at last, albeit a bit circuitously, the feeling inside me was sweet and had a deliciously victorious quality about it.

Being a writer myself, I am thrilled to no end to share the same creative, self-integrative path with the likes of James Thurber. We both learned to find our own voice, to channel our inner wisdom in an outward expression that we could share wholeheartedly and creatively with others. There is a security within ourselves, about who we are, that was hard won and relentlessly tempered by life.

Those early years were very challenging - not experiences I would wish to repeat. Yet at the same time, I would not change them even if I could. I have learned how to see the real me. I have learned to grow beyond where others cannot see me at all. I have reached within myself and found a woman of depth, character, sensitivity and wisdom. I have had a lifetime of practice accepting myself, flaws and all. I have learned to embrace and love my inner "freak." This cyclops has become a person of self-knowledge and entrenched self-confidence, immune to the poison of the slings and arrows (and rocks) of outrageous fortune and the erosion of toxic judgments.

What I considered an aesthetic liability growing up, not to mention a social death sentence, actually turned out to be my greatest developmental asset. Today I teach workshops at the most prestigious retreat centers in the world and I am a syndicated radio show host with a call-in program where listeners ask for guidance and clarity in their personal lives. I love having a life of service, helping others to overcome obstacles that are limiting their growth and personal happiness. This birth defect, along with other life challenges, has provided me with the best "on the job" training available, giving me the innate ability to extend compassion, support and sage advice to others. I have the talent and wisdom to empower my audiences to change their perspective and reframe their lives, allowing them to deal, in a healthy manner, with whatever surprises life throws their way.

Whenever I'm out and about and encounter other women in the flow of my everyday life, whether I'm traveling, standing in the line at the bank or cruising the isles of the grocery store, I pass out "Beyond Karma Queen" stickers. When ladies ask me what that means, I always answer, "Instead of trying to decide if the amount of cellulite you have is good or bad, wouldn't you rather just be beyond it?" I no longer try to figure out if the pain of being different is good or bad. Instead, I simply choose to just grow beyond the suffering imbedded within it. At this point in my life, some fifty years later, I see these earlier traumatizing events as the catalytic influences that have allowed me to claim my "Beyond Karma Queen" status. The cyclops, at long last, has gained authentic, life enhancing second sight.

Top Ten Tips for Surviving The Break Up of A Cheating Partner

*T*here is nothing about growing beyond the pain of a cheating partner that I fail to understand. As a personal growth professional, I often draw upon my own life experience to help others regain their footing, and reconnect to a life worth living. These are my hard won tips for surviving the break up.

1. Don't beat yourself up. Your cheating partner has most likely already done enough of that for the both of you. Beating yourself up can easily become a habit, so it needs to be avoided right from the start. If Christie Brinkley's recent divorce has taught women anything, it is that no matter how attractive, smart or successful you are, you are not immune. Partners cheat because of *their* insecurities, not because you are not good enough. When the urge arises to blame yourself for your partner's infidelities, it is imperative that you develop the habit of focusing on more life sustaining actions.

2. Don't dwell on the details of the infidelity. There is nothing you can do about what happened in the past. Dwelling on it only causes emotional scarring. It is impossible to focus on growing beyond your pain while simultaneously obsessing about what is creating your pain. The negativity will cancel out any gains you may have made to "grow beyond." You have free will over what you give your attention to. Healing requires that you use your free will to liberate yourself from the tyranny of suffering that an unfaithful partner inflicted upon your life. When you find yourself repeatedly visualizing your partner cheating, displace that ugliness by focusing on your next steps.

3. Change your image of yourself. Use this as an opportunity to reinvent yourself. Give yourself permission to let everything about yourself that you do not feel good about dissolve with the shattered relationship. If you noticed that you developed bad habits, such as making yourself small or powerless in your last relationship, resolve that issue and take your power back. You now have the space and freedom to be a new you. The mold is broken and it is time for you to claim the person and happiness you have always wanted. You do not have to settle for anything less.

4. Make time for yourself. This is a healing time: pamper and love yourself. There is no replacement for you loving yourself. The most reliable person to depend on to love you through difficult and challenging times is you. Balance the pain you are feeling with lavishing loving kindness upon yourself; a gentleness that no one can betray or can take away from you.

5. Focus on those that *do* support you - your relationships with family and friends. Ask for extra TLC from the relationships that have your best interest at heart. Let others know what your needs are, and let them give to you.

6. Don't isolate yourself. It's easy to hole up with a romance novel, or movie and a few pints of Ben & Jerry's. Contracting will only make the pain worse. This is a time to expand into a new life unfettered by a toxic, cheating partner. Get out there and start living life.

7. Acknowledge your new strength. This ordeal should have made you much wiser and stronger. This is one of life's many experiences, so learn from it. Validate your inner knowing and acknowledge your evolution into a wiser and more discerning person. You have already paid the price for this wisdom, so claim it! Don't let it get lost in the shuffle.

8. Focus only on what you want. Don't give your attention to negative issues: what you are praying will not happen. Every time you find yourself letting the worst case scenario run away with your attention, bring your point of focus back to giving attention singularly to what you *desire*. You will lose a lot of precious healing energy whenever you let your mind drift off to things that do not empower you.

9. Everything grows better with compost. Don't be excrementally challenged. Consider this a growth accelerant, not a failure. This experience comes complete with tons of emotional waste. Make sure it works for your growth; that is its greatest potential. Think of all the other painful events you have lived through that made you more loving and compassionate. This is no different.

10. Reposition yourself for the next phase of your new life. It can be an exciting, freeing and inspiring new life if you choose it. This iceberg does not have to sink your ship; you are not the Titanic. Do not give your cheating partner the power to send you to the bottom of the ocean. You and you alone are the architect of your own life. Draw on this to give yourself a strong, clear foundation for building a grander and greater life. As Gandhi says, "Be the change you wish to see."

Sociopath Recovery:

How To Take Your Power Back And Look Good Doing It

I had yet another conversation, with yet another friend, who found themselves reeling from an intimate relationship with yet another sociopath predator. Is it just me or has the human landscape, for whatever reason, become more and more littered with people that simply have not developed a conscience?

The story is typical: the sociopath was married yet claimed he was not. The sociopath falsely claimed he had cancer, so he could travel with impunity between the people he strung along. He was charming; he ingratiated himself to the entire family and their circle of friends. If anyone in the family questioned his behavior or came close to connecting the dots on his rampant deceit, the sociopath would become outraged and shift blame onto his intended victim. He spouted poisonous lies every time he opened his mouth. And, of course, it's a "given" that the sociopath had no remorse for the trail of human destruction he left in his wake and actually enjoyed knowing his activities were twisting a knife that would leave permanent scars.

Not only have I heard this story before, but I also have a couple to tell myself - life experiences I racked up here in the planet Earth classroom. Even without knowing their personal situations, I could recite chapter and verse how these people got caught up in the web that the sociopath weaves so well. I also know the anguish and deep-seated feelings of pain and betrayal that one goes through when the whole house of cards finally collapses and realization that the person who claimed to love you the most is as toxic as a meltdown at a nuclear reactor.

It is not my intention to give a lot of exposure to the sociopaths in our brief time together. There is a lot of great information available these days about their profile and how to spot them. One of the best out there is the Martha Stout, PhD book: *The Sociopath Next Door: The Ruthless Versus The Rest Of Us*. What I want to do is focus instead on how to go about picking up the pieces after the sociopath bomb has exploded in your life. There are many different "types" of sociopath, but I am going to focus on recovery from the love, or romantic sociopath predator relationship. Here are a few simple but extremely powerful tips I learned the hard way. I feel compelled to share these with you if for no other reason than to equalize the playing field.

Number One: The sociopath predators love tearing your world and especially your self-esteem to shreds. They revel in the knowledge that they are destroying you in ways that can be undetectable. The most crucial thing to bear in mind when taking your life and power back from these insidious, conscienceless forces of destruction is *don't beat yourself up!* The sociopath predator has already done a professional job of just that. You are the only person with a conscience and functional moral compass in this equation. You are the sole force of integrity and honesty in this mix. You have suffered enough! You have to stop the madness and not continue to forge a path through self-inflicted brutality. You are probably bludgeoning yourself with questions like: "How could I have not seen this coming?" Answer: You would have if you didn't have a conscience as well. The rest of us don't think in such deliberately distorted and diseased ways. Question: "Shouldn't I have connected the dots earlier and trusted in my inner knowing?" Answer: This experience is how you are learning to do just that. Do you blame a child for not knowing how to walk straight out of the womb? Of course not. This experience has solidified the ethereal process of trusting in your gut instinct – your feeling/knowing. This is your right of passage in becoming an expert at sensing, knowing and trusting in the red flags as they appear in the field of reality from this time forward. Now you know when something does not feel right or look right in a way that no one is going to be able to talk you out of. The gift, amidst all of this rubble, is that you now have an embodied galvanized self-corrective guidance system you can trust in and rely on.

Your job from here on out is to end the reign of hostility in your life. That includes the self-inflicted variety as well. There is no reason to continue hurting yourself and picking up where the sociopath left off after that predator has been ousted. Sociopaths, by nature, have no conscious. But they know you do, and they are masters at using yours against you. The biggest pitfall left to extricate yourself from is that of shame. There is nothing a sociopath predator loves more than to know you are crumbling under the strain of shame, guilt and self-loathing for violations they committed. In the name of growing beyond that ever-constricting snare, I want to share a great acronym for shame I recently came across at www.lovefraud.com/blog/2012/01/06/letters-to-lovefraud-to-the-liar-named-shame/: Self Hatred Accepting My Enslavement. Shame is a physiological/emotional booby trap the sociopath predator leaves behind. Don't step in it; do not deploy it. Defuse, dismantle and discard it.

Number Two: You have to make your mind like Teflon when the habit to re-visit and re-live the details of all the lies, cheating and manipulations resurfaces in your memory. Let that ugly energy slide right off of you. Nothing sticks because you are too busy refocusing on your new life - meeting new, wonderful and caring people. You have cleaned up your relationship space. You now have room to invite in and bond with like-minded people of integrity and compassion.

Deny the sociopath predator any further power in your life. Every time you shrink back in fear that you can no longer trust people, you give your power away to the sociopath predator yet again. You have to choose that they no longer get a say in the quality of your life. They no longer get to influence the potential of how free and expansive your experience of life can be. This is the time to take to heart the Satchel Page quote, "Work like you don't need the money. Dance like no one is watching. Love like you have never been hurt." This is how you take back your power, your life and your peace of mind!

Every time you slip back into that noxious quagmire of reflection on the bondage of pain, stop! Instead, focus on what you *do* want. Focus on the life you came here to live, not the existence you wish to grow beyond. Focus on the loving caring relationships you do have, be it your animal companion, friends, or even your sense of humor. Don't succumb to the sociopath's will; the best revenge is living well. You have to take your mind back and make it your best friend and not your second worst enemy. You have made it through the graduate class in learning how to trust in yourself. Now is the time to go out and live the life you just paid a very hefty price for.

Number Three: For those of you who feel that spirituality still has something viable and life sustaining to offer, please consider this: many, many people have died and returned to tell about the experience - commonly know as an NDE (near death experience). The consistent element in these personal accounts is what is referred to as the life review. When a person dies, they see their life in a review. But it is not like watching your life like one would view a movie. In the life review you relive your life from the viewpoint of those around you. And, you not only see your life events, you feel them too. For example, if you were a schoolyard bully, in your life review you would now feel what it was like to be on the receiving end of your violence.

What could you ever do to a sociopath predator that is worse than turning the tables and having them now suffer through the pain and misery they so joyously delivered into your life? They will ultimately get away with nothing. They will be tortured and tormented to the same exacting degree that you were, without escape, without reprieve, without exception. You do not have to do anything but get on with your new life. No need to soil your own hands, just focus on the good and life-sustaining opportunities you have for growth and personal happiness.

Number Four: Remember, this all about you moving forward as a wiser more aware person as a result of graduating from this relationship. Leave the bitterness behind. It will not serve you in creating a life worth living. The only thing that matters now is loving and nurturing yourself through the grief and the shock. The greater the new and improved version of your life is, the happier and more resilient you are. And, the more powerless and meaningless the sociopath predator will become.

Keep focusing on what you do want. When the habit to look back sneaks up on you, keep your eye on the prize: keep putting one emotional foot in front of the other and commit yourself to moving forward. No one will be able to talk you out of your power again. You now recognize the inner alarm of deception whether or not you can actually put your finger on what exactly seems wrong.

The Universe at large will take care of educating the sociopath predator. It is no longer your problem. Just create the best possible life review for yourself that is humanly and Divinely possible. There is a new life that awaits you. Find it, live it, celebrate it, claim it. You deserve it!

Failure To Communicate
Not a Cool Hand

I never met Hal in person; we only spoke over the phone. My publicity people introduced us via email and thought we would be kindred spirits. There were times over the next four to five years when Hal and I might talk almost every day. And then, due my traveling schedule, there would be times we would not speak for a few weeks. Hal was very well educated and loved sharing what he knew with others. He was the editor of "Quest" magazine. He was a 33-degree Free Mason. He was also a very loyal and devoted son, brother and friend. As my publicity people already knew, Hal was extremely knowledgeable about a myriad of topics and he became a frequent guest on my radio show, "You Are What You Love©."

About a year or more into our on-going phone relationship, Hal revealed to me that he was very concerned about his health. He made this burdensome confession shortly after his brother had been found dead in his hotel room, while waiting for a liver transplant. Although Hal was never totally revealing about his health, I was able to fill in some of the blanks from his descriptions of symptoms he would disclose from time to time. I was constantly encouraging him to seek out professional medical treatment. I even offered to fly to his home, a hotel room, and take him by the hand and get him set up with some responsible medical protocol. But Hal would have none of it. He was scared. He was frightened he would be given the same diagnosis as his now deceased brother. He was afraid he would not be able to qualify for health insurance, his illness would be deemed a pre-existing condition, and he would be rejected when he most needed life saving support. He was terrified to die, while simultaneously reluctant to commit to living. Hal was convinced that life had nothing to offer him but more suffering, disappointment and deep disconcerting apprehension.

Hal's brother had died alone in an extend stay hotel room. And ironically, Hal spent the last four years of his life living at the same extended stay hotel chain. Maybe they should advertise as "The Next Best Thing to Hospice." Hal was like a pearl of wisdom trapped inside this hard clamshell of impenetrable fear. We frequently talked about simple things he could do to start incorporating into his life a routine of diet, exercise and life-style changes that would contribute to a more life-sustaining foundation. Hal always listened politely and patiently, often ending our prolonged conversations with, "You know sweetie, when we hang up, that is exactly what I'm going do." However, I eventually learned Hal was neither willing nor interested in following up on any of the suggestions we ever discussed. The bottom line was Hal simply did not want to leave his hotel room. The longer he sat there the more he convinced himself the insulation of that hotel room offered the best quality of life he was ever going to find. Or at least he was safer and better off than subjecting himself to the uncertainty and harsh realities that lay waiting to ambush him in the cold unfeeling world just outside of that hotel room door.

No matter how hard all of Hal's friends collectively and individually tried to coax him out of that emotional tar pit of fear and into proactive movement, Hal resisted with an equal and opposite display of energy. It was as if the spirit of Sisyphus had possessed his Soul. No matter how close I felt we had gotten to rolling his burden of fear aside so he could liberate himself from a perennial uphill battle with self-inflicted terror, that stone would ultimately roll back down in front of his hotel room door in the time it took to hang up the phone.

The last time I spoke with Hal I knew he would most likely not last the week. He had successfully sentenced himself to death - a prisoner of fear living in solitary on death row in his hotel cell. He had practiced this contraction so vehemently, that he had to be physically carried from his hotel room to the hospital where he died not long afterwards.

The evening of Hal's funeral service the movie "Cool Hand Luke" was airing. I had seen the movie countless times before. There is something irresistible about the draw of Paul Newman combined with the charisma of one Luke Jackson that calls to viewers like the sirens of Ulysses. It is the ultimate film opiate. For obvious reasons Hal was looming large in my mind. The more I watched the movie, the more I realized there was a striking similarity between the lives and deaths of Hal and Luke.

Both Hal and Luke found themselves "incarcerated" by engaging in actions they both knew would solve nothing in the bigger picture of their lives. But they were at a loss as to a better or more meaningful way to communicate. Both wanted out of the situation they found themselves in, without ever having to deal with the inner issues that landed them in that confined space in the first place. Both had a deep-seated driven need to know that there is more to life than what one can see, touch, taste and smell. Like Cool Hand Luke, Hal was someone you wanted to hang out with; you were a better person as a result of time spent together. They were both people who inspired you to question and explore a different direction, sometimes out of nothing more than their own sheer stubbornness. Both of them had a cruel and unrelenting warden that tracked them down without mercy and without rest. Hal's warden was the voice of fear that destroyed his every attempt to escape his jail cell, thinly disguised as an extended stay hotel room. Luke's warden was equally barbarically unappeasable, reminding him at every failed escape attempt that, "What we have here is failure to communicate." And finally both of them were unsuccessful at negotiating their way free.

The irony amidst all this similarity is that both were stuck as polar opposites. Hal could not move to literally save his own life. He decreed and re-enforced a self-imposed life sentence of imprisonment and nothing could bring him out of it. Luke, on the other hand, could not stop running. To the degree to which Hal was paralyzed, Luke was equally possessed by the urge to bust loose. Hal would not move to solve his life-threatening problems and Luke would not sit still to resolve his. Could either of these men have been more bull headed or predictable in their choices? And of course, sadly, both men found their lives ending early by way of the same self-perpetuated undeterrable form of self-destruction.

The more the comparison between Hal and Luke became self-evident, the more I realized how much we all have a little Hal and a little Luke within us. All of us, at some time or another, have found ourselves unwilling to get out of our own way: either by refusing to hold still when we need to face something or by purposefully remaining stagnant when we know that life and everyone we care about is passing us by.

As Oscar Wilde put it, "Life imitates art far more than art imitates life." Luke is a fictional personality. Hal is not. Whether we strive to free ourselves from ourselves for real or for imagined reasons the action that is of paramount importance is that we must be willing to show up for the challenge and the process, without running away or hiding. Now, the unanswered question of whether we take that action by holding our ground or by a committed movement forward is one each of us has to answer personally within the context of our own hearts and lives. One thing is for certain, when we avoid personal growth by either extreme measures of denial or by a heighten need to constantly escape, what we inevitably get is the definitive "failure to communicate" a life worth living within ourselves. I trust that Hal and Luke will live large in our hearts and minds as the ironic symbols for both "stubborn single-mindedness" and "it is never too late to change."

In Loving Memory of Hal Garland Siemer (June 14, 1958 - July 17, 2011).

Mosque'd in Controversy

*R*ecently there has been so much time and energy given to the topic of building a mosque near the site of the Twin Towers, that it would be a shame to allow the opportunity for greater understanding to pass by without further examination.

It has been argued that this is an issue of judging and discriminating against an entire religious group due to the sociopathic actions of a select few, who were more politically motivated than anything else. If we put this "religious issue" in historical perspective, it changes the context. Hitler, a self-professed practicing Christian, committed atrocities on a much greater scale. His "final solution" was a crime of the most extreme religious bias. But at no time did anyone suggest that the construction of Christian churches be stopped because it honors Hitler or any other infamous, self-proclaimed, crime committing Christians. Somehow we recognize that as myopic and small minded.

There are zealots in every religious sect. It is a personal trait, not a religious characteristic. Punishing all the Muslims is no different than the Nazi's punishing all Jews. Not all Germans were Nazis and not all Muslims are terrorists. We do not want to lose sight of the important question here: who is the enemy? Are all the Americans of German ancestry who fought in WWII the enemy? What about the Americans of Japanese ancestry in-carcerated in internment camps? And, on a not so global level, what about all the serial killers who claimed God told them to kill? God even told Abraham to kill his first-born son, which not only sets a precedent, but also adds credibility to the others. We haven't stopped those who openly practice communicating with God because of the crimes of a few deeply emotionally ill people. We know better than that. So who is the real enemy here? Is it Islam? No. It is a small group of extremists cowardly hiding behind Islam to justify the indefensible.

Most people do not know that there is already a mosque that is only four blocks away from ground zero. It is in a building that predates the Twin Towers. If we start censoring where people can build a house of worship, where do we stop? How many blocks away will be far enough? And what about mosques that existed before the Twin Towers were built but are now consid-ered too close to a sensitive landmark? Do we raze them because we find their very existence offensive? And what about free will? Are the builders of this proposed mosque subject to different laws than anyone else following their heart in a land where they are proclaimed constitutionally free to do so?

Loving and caring for each other is the highest philosophical, moral, ethical and religious teaching in the Universe. America is a predominately Judeo/Christian country. We give aggressive lip service to valuing this ethical "love thy neighbor" compassion-based philosophical standard. Yet it is those people practicing religious beliefs based on the ethical gold standard of tolerance, compassion and forgiveness that are the ones protesting with the most vitriol. Do these same people protest that all Muslims should be denied access to Heaven? After all, how could Heaven permit any Souls from Islam to enter? It would be too offensive to the Souls who died in the Twin Towers to have to share paradise with them. And if growing beyond limitation, fear and hate is what Heaven is all about, how can we co-create manifesting Heaven on Earth if we practice a way of life that clearly violates the Spirit of Heaven and peace on Earth?

As prominent as religious hypocrisy is in this debate, there is a deeper issue. Responding to others in a manner the unifies everyone, respects the free will of others and honors the sacredness of all life, regardless of the "outer label," is what the potential of this affair is truly about. Forget what religion the people who crashed into the Twin Towers claimed to be, for their actions represent them more accurately than their dogma. Clearly their real religion is disrespectful to human life and based on a love of hatred and mindless destruction. The Twin Towers attack was designed to divide our unity as a people and as a nation. The terrorist have accomplished their mission all these years later, if we allow ourselves to focus on the negative and dwell on how that single event continues to fracture and divide instead of unify and heal us.

The real tragedy is if we participate in creating further division and separation within our own minds and communities. The danger we need to be aware of here is not the scrutiny of religions associated with terroristic acts. It is not where a mosque is or is not built. It is the twisted and distorted concept that democracy is somehow served by justifying an argument of isolation and hatred. If we allow that to happen, we destroy democracy from the inside out.

When a bully intimidates you, that bully expects a certain reaction from you, his victim. That bully wants you to behave in a manner he is coercing. If you give away your power to that bully, he wins. Now is the time to stand our ground, in solidarity, and take our power back. This is the time to say, "No matter what happens to us, we are unconditionally the land of the free and the home of the brave. We do not recognize any other power: not the power of intimidation, fear, divisiveness, intolerance or bigotry. No matter what the world throws at us, we stand as one, and 9/11 only has the ability to makes us stronger and more resilient."

When we choose to let the conduct of others divide us, we lose something infinitely greater than the Twin Towers and those who perished that day. We lose sight of ourselves as free, brave people. We undermine our individual and collective dignity; we erode our inner relationship with integrity; we corrupt our knowing of ourselves as sovereign. But most importantly, we compromise what we value most of all... the experience of ourselves as the greatest experiment in human freedom the planet has ever seen.

The reductionist fixation on the location of a building is distracting us from a bigger picture problem which is essentially *how do we see ourselves?* How do we *choose* to define and perceive ourselves? It would be a tragedy of the greatest proportion to permit the work of a few terrorists to set the parameters of our self-knowing and self-actualizing. Allowing the actions of a few to skew and contort this critical point of focus is not what free, brave people choose.

Where a mosque is or is not built should not have the power to define us. A building is an inanimate structure that only has the meaning we imbue upon it with our thoughts and beliefs. If we choose to see ourselves as broken, victimized and wounded, we will see life through the filter of fear and outrage. We can take our power back and liberate ourselves from the gyrations of the outer world by choosing inwardly to see ourselves as free, brave people who have the power individually and collectively to grow beyond anything that has hurt us.

Saying "I Do" to Gay Marriage: It's Just Good Business

I don't normally consider actor/comedian Tom Arnold a disseminator of sage wisdom, yet in his recent appearance on Conan O'Brien's now defunct *Tonight Show*, he surprised me with a rather enlightened perspective. Tom was talking about the highly charged issue of gay marriage when out of the blue he pointed out the most obvious and yet collectively overlooked epiphany. Arnold started out with a statement that completely transcended all religious dogma and political ideology: "I appeal to your sense of greed." Gay marriage... it simply makes good business sense.

Consider that most same sex couples do not have children to drain any trace of disposable income from their bank accounts. To quote Sam Austin, "Homosexuality is God's way of insuring that the truly gifted aren't burdened with children." In addition a majority of these relationships are two income households. How could all the florists, caterers, photographers, stretch limo drivers, high-end venues, designer label clothiers, jewelers and wedding planners have missed this one? We are talking big ticket spenders here! Remember Liza Minnelli's last wedding? $3.5 million. It was the envy of every gay couple. Just envision mini versions of this gold splashed, fairy tale, no expense spared (and you thought I was going to say, "No holes barred") wedding orgy scattered across this financially starved country. Small business owners everywhere would put on their sequined outfits and dance around the ATM machine shouting, "Fabulous! Marvelous! Work it baby, work it!"

And the lawyers, my God, how could we forget the lawyers! I'm surprised they haven't already formed their own special lobby to push gay marriages through the legislative process in record time. Look at all the money they stand to make on everything from prenuptial agreements to long, drawn out custody battles over who pays for little Merlot the Chihuahua's massages and grooming and who gets visitation rights on holidays and weekends. The income that lawyers rake in from heterosexual marriages gone awry is immeasurable. It has evolved into a legal specialty unto itself. Why limit your clientele? Like same sex couples won't get messy divorces? When Tom Arnold first uttered those immortal words, "Let me appeal to your greed," it should have been like a drop of blood in a shark tank to every divorce attorney in the land.

And let's not forget the fees and taxes involved here as well. Marriage license? $50 give or take. Good thing it doesn't come with an expiration date…then again, maybe not. Sales taxes would be collected first on services such as engagement parties, hotel rooms, airplane tickets, dinners, jewelry, weddings, liquor, clothes purchased and formal attire rented, and then on divorce proceedings, Vegas annulments, restraining orders, pet detectives and the list goes on. And, assuming all these businesses pay their income taxes… well, you do the math. Why, gay marriage alone could underwrite the entire healthcare program.

Ask any wedding related business out there (and trust me there are a multitude) if they really care if their next big spending client is gay or straight, and I suspect the answer you would get most frequently would be, "As long as their credit is good, who cares?" Or, assessing the economic aspect in military terms, "Don't ask, don't tell, doesn't matter." Unfortunately, what is lost economically is only incidental to our greater loss.

Up until now, we have correlated consumers and business owners on this issue, but we have ignored the aspect of how we are all inter-related as a nation and as a people. Whenever we make it illegal for any group of people to be treated with dignity and respect, it costs us all, everywhere, in every imaginable way. We all lose something when any one group is targeted as not worthy of receiving basic human rights. No matter what the reason, this cannot be justified. But leave it to comics and late night talk show hosts to tease out the basic common denominator that hits us in our most sensitive spot... our wallets!

The level of hypocrisy in this controversy is absolutely toxic. We trust gay people to teach our children, even adopt and raise children, perform life saving surgeries, serve as police officers, pilot airplanes, rescue people from burning buildings and fight our wars. Yet at the same time, we deny them the simple right to legally protect their union with a loved one? We allow women, nuns, to marry "God." That is not even a marriage within the same dimension, although you could call it a match made in Heaven. At what time did we all vote on that? But we do not allow gay marriage? We pretend all people are created equally, but we do not live that self-evident truth.

There is a saying in the gay community, "Dorothy, lose the dress;

keep the shoes!" I suspect there is great wisdom there when applied correctly. In the case for gay marriage, "Lose the prejudice; keep the economy." People looking to share in the equality of the American dream, while spending cold hard cash during an economic recession, seems like a no brainer. Finally, a union everyone can agree on.

How To Clear &
Detoxify Crystals

*A*ll crystals are extremely efficient, natural amplifiers. That is why they are integral components of turntables, watches and computers. For thousands of years crystals have been used for healing purposes as well, and for the exact same reason modern technology uses them: they amplify energy. If you come in contact with a crystal for any reason, it will amplify your energy. It doesn't matter if you are touching it for healing, wearing it as a piece of jewelry or just admiring it.

Crystals also retain some of the energy they are exposed to. Every person who has ever been in physical contact with that crystal, from the mining process, to the cutting and polishing, to the retailers who sold the crystal and everyone in between has added their energy to the amplification mix. When crystals are used in healing, one of the primary issues has always been how to "clean" a crystal of all of this retained energy. Why might that be a problem you might ask? Because the crystal is now amplifying everyone's energy that has ever touched it and that may not be healthy, balancing or appropriate to keep in your house, around your neck, on your finger or in your healing room.

Let's say you inherited some jewelry from your Auntie Em in Kansas: a lovely diamond ring, an opal necklace and an amethyst bracelet. As you are admiring the passed on articles, you cannot help but remember what a nasty, mean-spirited, judgmental person Aunt Em was. Her energy is still in that jewelry; it did not die with her. When you wear that jewelry it has an amplified energetic effect on your life.

If you picked up some great deals at an estate sale, you probably have no idea if the previous owner(s) had a nasty personality, or suffered from a long-term illness such as cancer or possibly died traumatically while wearing some the very same items now in your possession. Any of these circumstances could have an adverse effect on your health. Amplified energy does not live in a vacuum. It does not neutralize itself automatically simply because the mineral has found a new home. Crystals continue to store and accumulate all the energy they have ever been exposed to until they are cleared.

In the same manner that you would never consider wearing or adding a garment to your wardrobe that someone else had worn for many years without washing it first, the same applies to crystals. Every new gem, mineral or fossil you acquire needs to be cleared of the energy imprint made on it by the previous owner(s) and anyone who has ever touched or handled that stone. There are many commonly used methods to energetically clean a crystal: covering it with salt or salt water, burying it in the ground, placing it in the sunlight or moonlight or smudging it, otherwise known as surrounding it with the smoke of burning sage. However, Indian Ayurvedic wisdom says that none of these methods are actually proficient in neutralizing all the energy any crystal has picked up and stored. The Ayurvedic, time-honored method of clearing any stone is to place it in a container and cover it with organic, whole milk. The only exception to the milk mineral detoxification technique is azurite and azurite-malachite (do not soak these stones). You can place more than one item in a container before covering with milk, as long as all the items to be cleared are thoroughly and completely submerged in the milk. Remember, the gems and minerals are not on a fat-free diet. You want to use whole organic milk for the best cleansing results. After covering the items to be cleared with milk, let them sit for twenty-four hours. Then wash off the items and place them in a clean container and cover with milk again. Repeat the process for a total of three full days.

On the third day thoroughly rinse the milk off the stones and dry them completely. You will find the gems and minerals are now not only cleared energetically but also have an enhanced dazzling quality of brilliance. Unless you have submerged a very intricately detailed piece of sterling silver, with lots of little crevices, you will also find that your entire jewelry item is brighter and lovelier than ever. Also be careful not to soak items strung on silk or string, as the milk over the three-day soak will start to disintegrate the cord. It does not matter if you leave the soaking stones in or out of the refrigerator over the three-day period. What is important is that you make sure that no animals, such as a cat or dog, drink the milk containing detoxified energy from the stones. So if you have to, place the container in the fridge to make sure your pet does not have access to the toxic milk. Also make sure the used milk is completely washed down the drain and not reused.

The best time to clean any gem, mineral or fossil is immediately after it comes into your possession. If you use crystals or stones for healing, such as a hot stone massage, it is best to soak that crystal or stone in milk for three days before using on another person. Also remember anytime someone else handles your gems and minerals it now has their energy in the mineral. So if you loan out your jewelry, be sure to soak it in milk for three days when you get it back. If people are shaking your hand and your rings and bracelets come into contact with others, you may want to cleanse your jewelry once a month. There is no limit to how many times you can cleanse a crystal or how many crystals you can clear at one time, as long as the milk completely covers every gem and mineral.

Over the years I have maintained this practice, it never fails to astound me how dramatically brighter and oftentimes clearer a stone can become after soaking in milk for three days. It is a simple, cost effective method and the results are well worth the time and the effort. It is energetically the perfect way to love and protect your gems and minerals as much as they love and enhance your life.

Body

Staying in Focus

*E*verything is energy. Atoms vibrating at different frequencies form matter. In the physical world the only thing separating a chair from a rock is their rate of vibration. Even nonphysical entities such as thoughts, memories, feelings, love and fear are forms of energy with their own frequency and magnetic signature as well.

The Eastern sciences of self-healing say that all illness first starts on a vibrational energy level. In other words the energy body affects the physical body, not the other way around. The subtle energies that form the body are dis-at-ease long before a measurable disease shows up in the slower, energetically denser physical body. Allopathic doctors are not trained to diagnose from an energy level. They only monitor the physical body. This is why most doctors cannot see what is actually happening until a full-blown medical crisis has manifested. This is also how Ayurvedic doctors and Doctors of Oriental Medicine, who monitor the body's energy patterns, can "see" a health problem long before it shows up in a blood test, MRI or CAT scan. Ayurvedic practitioners and Doctors of Oriental Medicine are trained to diagnose the patient's energy by reading the pulse, looking at the person's eyes, hair, skin, emotional reactions and body type. All these forms of diagnostic information gathering allow the alternative practitioner the ability to understand how the patient's energy intelligence is organized before it solidifies in the body.

Awareness, what are we giving our attention to, is the most life altering form of energy available to us. It is our awareness that has the greatest influence on the body, our perceptions and emotions. Eastern psychologies say that emotions are attracted to the body's nervous system according to what the person is giving their attention to. Thus the emotional body actually reacts to the consciousness body. Your anger is the emotional body's response to your thoughts; your thoughts do not take their cues from your emotions.

The other energies that make up the human experience do not live in a vacuum either. For example, when it comes to the physical body, the Eastern sciences of self-healing say that over 95% of all illness and weakness within the body have an emotional origin. The sequence is: thoughts attract emotions that, if unresolved, may cause physical problems. Unresolved emotions build up and become increasingly exacerbated by what you habitually give your attention to. Thoughts fuel the emotional fire. The inner narrative and dialogue you are running, your so-called "story," attracts toxic emotions that in turn accumulate in the body and poison it, if you do not release them. If you keep reliving a negative experience, or one your awareness considers negative, it will make you sick. So please, acknowledge emotions as they come up; then release that vibration and let the emotions go. You know, "Get over it!"

Every cause and effect leads back to what you are giving your attention to. Knowing this, I titled my first book and radio shows "You Are What You Love©," which is the short version of the Spiritual Law: *you are what you love, and you love whatever you are giving your attention to*. All the energies that make up physical human life are fundamentally organized and vibrate according to what you give your attention to and how you feel about what you give your attention to. The body, emotions and perceptions are giving you the results they are under the impression you want based exclusively on your awareness. Awareness can be the gateway to health or illness based on… you guessed it, what you are giving your attention to.

Since imbalance and disease enter through the doorway of awareness, they can also be ushered out through the power of that same portal. When you give your attention to things that live in an unlimited, high vibrational realm such as gratitude, acceptance, love and forgiveness, you have contact with the other Spiritual Beings that also live in those unlimited realms. This means if you are seeking Angelic intervention in your life for whatever reason, giving your attention to things that reside in the same dominion as the Angelic community is the most potent way to usher that relationship into direct contact with your life.

When you seek Angelic interaction and then give your attention to things that live in a hellishly limited place, you remove yourself from receiving the support of that unlimited community. The idea is to make yourself accessible to Angelic services by staying in their presence, and this is done via what you are giving your attention to. Even if you are in pain, be it physical, emotional, financial or otherwise, you can ask for help and then gratefully acknowledge their Divine assistance. In your time of need see yourself as being treasured and adored by the Divine. By giving your attention to these unlimited things you remain firmly in the loving and healing hands of the Heavenly community.

The old saying "We have seen the enemy and it is us" has never been truer when it comes to what we habitually give our attention to. We invite, accumulate and aggravate our miseries according to what we give our attention to. Conversely we also heal, overcome and breakthrough life's challenges according to our awareness. The empowering aspect of this situation is that what lives in an unlimited, Heavenly place is only as far away as what we are focusing on.

Space: Mind/Body/Spirit's Final Frontier

*W*hat I love about the Eastern sciences of self-healing is their comprehensive approach to managing and understanding the human experience. For example, in our accepted paradigm here in the West, "health" is considered the absence of illness. I cannot even begin to express how myopically offensive that is from an Eastern point-of-view. In reality, illness starts out very slowly, gradually moving out of balance with subtle energies that don't even register on most people's awareness radar. From an Indian, Tibetan Ayurvedic and Chinese Medicine paradigm everything is energy in motion or in stasis. These sciences specialize in examining how the subtle energies that organize your body's constitution are balanced:

- What are the qualities of these energies?

- What is the configuration of these energies?

- What and where are the energies in excesses

- What and where are the energies in deficiencies?

- What and where are these energies too dry, too hot, too wet or too cold?

Already you can see the conversation is straying from the familiar allopathic confines of a numbers game: weight, blood pressure, cholesterol count, etc.

Very simply stated, the Eastern self-healing sciences see illness as having its origins in an energetic make-up that could pre-exist for years before any actual physical symptoms arise. From an Eastern understanding there are subtle energies that make up any living being, be it the planet itself, a vegetable, an animal or a human. In Ayurveda these energies are: Air and Space (Vata), Fire and Water (Pitta), and Earth and Water (Kapha); in Chinese Medicine they are Earth, Water, Metal, Wood and Fire. Every living thing - animal, vegetable or mineral - has an energetic balance that is appropriate for its constitutional make up. This means that some people have more Fire energy than others; some people have more Earth energy than others; still others may have more Water or Air than others. Each living thing has a mixture of these energies that make up life in a unique formula that balances and supports that life form. In the same way that no two people have the same fingerprints, every living thing is organized with an energy blueprint specific to their exclusive individual existence.

> Let's build on this idea of energies coming together in a specific manner that determines your unique life construction. The beginning of illness, again from an Eastern perspective, is where one or more of these energies that make up your life experience begins to accumulate in excess. A Fire predominate person would have the following proclivities: you eat lots of hot spicy foods; you love your beer and/or wine; you have a tendency to express yourself on the critical, impatient, ir-

ritated end of the spectrum; you like to wear a lot of red, orange and yellow colors. In order for you to be happy, things need to be done in a certain way: in a clearly defined time frame; life better be organized in a specific manner; you are perfection oriented and have a keenly honed eye for detail that must be met or there will be no rest. All these things provoke the Fire element in your unique energy constitution. If this Fire energy is continually stoked, provoked and generally inflamed, the subtle energy of Fire will grow and grow and grow. Fire energy is expansive in nature, so it will steadily accumulate and accumulate until there is an excess of Fire energy in your body's constitution that cannot be maintained within the boundaries of balance and good health. (There may be more than just Fire involved too. For example, it may be Fire and excess Air energy that are building dramatically like a brush fire blown out of control by a strong wind.) They have now reached a level of aggravation to the body's system and delicate point of energy balance. Bear in mind all this may be happening while the individual is still relatively symptom free. This is the time so many people go to their doctor feeling/knowing something is not right, but the doctor cannot *find* anything amiss or diagnose a pathology. "Sorry, your tests came back negative. There is nothing wrong with you."

Once the out of balance energy or energies reach a level of profound and excessive accumulation, an aggravation flashpoint will occur. It is at this late stage that measurable symptoms will begin to arise. Since the imbalance has become a full-blown malady, allopathic test results will come back positive and Western medicine can make a diagnosis. Better late than never I guess. The obvious advantage goes to the system of self-healing that can detect and respond to the energy or energies while still in accumulation mode - long before it reaches critical mass and becomes a health crisis. However, accumulation and aggravation are only part of the overall picture that addresses balance, illness and wellbeing.

Once an accumulated energy (or energies) moves into aggravation mode, the excess aggravated energy will then go into the body's circulatory system and cycle around and around the body's overall structure. This empowered accumulated/aggravated energy circulates until it finds a "defective" space within the body. The accumulated/aggravated energy will then deposit itself in the "defective" space. This is what is known in the Eastern systems of self-healing as the manifestation of a full-scale disease. So this raises the $64 million dollar question.... what exactly is a "defective" space, and if you did not have any "defective" spaces would there be any inner fertile ground for disease to take root?

Let's take these on one at a time. What is a defective space? This is where the mind/body connection comes to the forefront of discussion. A defective space starts in the mind; it is created by what you give your attention to and the emotions that arise as a result of that awareness. These Eastern systems of self-healing define you as a spiritual being having a human experience. They see you as inseparable from a force of consciousness that existed before you came here and took a body, and will continue to exist as consciousness after the body falls away. They do not take your spiritual identity out of the health equation. Western medicine, on the other hand, at no time even acknowledges you as anything other than a mechanism. They fail to address the mind, body, spirit connection that exists.

Socrates said it best: "The unexamined life is not worth living." The purpose of all created life is to experience the truth of who we are, and to honestly examine what we are and why we are here. When you define yourself as inferior, less than, not good enough, unlovable, worthless, disposable or powerless, you create a "defective" space in the mind/body energy configuration. The reason for this is because those thoughts are in direct opposition to who and what you are. They create a relationship of dis-ease between you and the truth that promotes balance and sets you free. Nature does not like a vacuum so when you give your power away and create a "defective" space, the pain, trauma and toxic energy that pushed *you* out, moves in.

When you love, accept and forgive yourself for the learning experiences you agreed to go through and take on, in order to become self-realizing and self-aware, you heal these "defective" spaces in the mind and body. Self-loathing, self-judgment and criticism erode inner integrity and personal balance until it leaves a "defective" space in its wake.

There is nothing stronger than a fully realized being. Disease is a measurable, tangible state of being dis-at-ease with your conscious knowledge of yourself, and the symptoms of that dis-at-ease state will ultimately manifest physically. Obviously everyone has entertained "defective" thinking to varying degrees. The objective of life in this planet Earth classroom is to grow beyond the habit of giving attention to "defective" consciousness and return to a place of self-acceptance, ease and wholeness. So to answer that $64 million dollar question: a "defective" space starts in the mind with attention given to an inner narrative based on a lack of self-acceptance, and then spreads to the body. If you did not have any "defective" spaces you would be immune to illness and disease… you also most likely would not be in the planet Earth classroom as there would be nothing for you to learn here. That is why everyone here has to learn to grow beyond toxic thinking and has experienced illness to some degree.

Even if you disagree with the fundamental concepts and principles shared here, let me ask you something. What do you have to lose by accepting yourself? How is the quality of your life compromised in the least by extending love, compassion and forgiveness to yourself?

But you do not have to take my word for it. Examine your own life. When you are comfortable, relaxed and confident within your own skin… don't you automatically feel better? At the end of the day you may not have full control over the amount of radiation, GMOs or environmental toxins you have been habitually exposed to, but you do have the last word on how you see yourself, how you define yourself, how feel about yourself and what you tell yourself. And *if* the only thing you have any real control over is limiting the amount of defective space in your own mind so that you feel better about yourself and your life at the end of the day… what is that worth to you?

What Is More Contagious Than Swine Flu?

H1N1 – R U OK?

*T*he only thing more highly contagious than a virus, bacteria, mold spore or free radical is fear. The panic that arises from imagining oneself succumbing to the dreaded swine flu is a far greater health-threatening condition. It travels much faster and with more drastic consequences than the actual illness itself, leaving its own trail of destruction in its perceptual wake. Maybe they should change the name of the swine flu from the H1N1 virus to the CNN#1 Ratings virus panic-demic. You know, we can't just sit around waiting for Homeland Security to kill all the free radicals so we can feel safe once again. And now I heard the pigs are worried about contracting the swine flu from humans! On top of that, I just don't look good wearing one of those respirator masks, not to mention that they don't make them in purple.

The Eastern systems of self-healing, Chinese Medicine, Indian and Tibetan Ayurveda all state that well over 95% of all illnesses have an emotional impetus or basis. It is not so much exposure to life's detrimental elements that begin the cause and effect chain reaction culminating in disease, so much as how we emotionally responded to those elements. The Eastern systems explain that the physical body itself is inherently neutral; but clearly the emotional body is not. The physical body not only takes its cues from what we think, but also, and most importantly, from how we *feel* about what we give our attention to. The physical body thus organizes its response to health and balance according to what it is under the impression that the mind and emotions want - what we give our attention to and how we feel about it. The body basically reads our minds.

Fear, worry and insecurity stress the emotional, mental and physical bodies, thereby weakening the body's immune system. When we imagine ourselves getting sick, the body is under the impression this is what we are expecting from it. The body sees us as self-identifying with this condition and will go out of its way to give us that result. The body is a lot like a rental car. It does not drive itself around; it is neutral. It is merely responding to the choices and attention of the driver.

Fear is a very contractive energy. Anyone who experiences fear will notice that their chest gets tight, breathing becomes shallow and muscles constrict. When the mind focuses on something that creates a panic response, the body will automatically contract around that stimulus; that is the nature of fear. Hence whatever we resist persists.

The body's strongest link in the immune defense system is the lymphatic system. Lymph is a fluid. Its oily, water-like consistency is how it pumps itself throughout the body, cleaning out viruses, bacteria even cancer cells before these potentially harmful elements can work their way deeper into the body. Skeletal muscles assist in pumping the lymph throughout the body. When muscles constrict from fear, these contractions bring the fluid to a screeching halt. The very last message a healthy person wants to send to the lymphatic system is one of stagnancy due to the contraction happening in the perceptual/emotional driver's seat.

If you imagine your body as recognizing what is life sustaining and ignoring every other influence, you give your body healthy and positive guidance around which it can organize its intelligence. For years researchers and doctors have known that having cancer patients visualize their white blood cells attacking and eliminating cancer cells improves the response of the immune system and increases a person's chances of survival. Telling your body that you trust it has the strength, energy and wisdom to eradicate any un-balancing foreign energy, be it a virus, bacteria or free radical will give your body confidence and clarity about exactly what response you expect from it when it encounters these elements.

Anyone who has participated in the fire walk knows the ability to stroll over hot embers without scorching one's feet is deter-mined and directed by what you are giving your attention to when initiating that first step forward. That is also the key to all of life. At any given moment, what are you giving your at-tention to? Are your choosing fear, or are you choosing love? You have free will. The media may be dispensing fear, but you decide whether or not you will accept that as your truth. If you cannot take your power back from CNN's frenetic fear-fest pan-demic panic, your body will be under the impression that you want contractive, fear-based responses - that you are choosing to learn more from fear before moving on to the love portion of the program. Your body will be operating within the fear-motivated navigational instructions of what you give your attention to, and allow any virus, bacteria or other potentially caustic energy that matches the vibration level of fear into your system; simply be-cause it is under the impression you want it. You set the param-eters; you are the driver; you set the course.

That should really make you want to clean up what you give your attention to! Again, the body is neutral. If you say, "Turn left into fear," the body will do just that. If you say, "Continue fearlessly forward," trusting you can grow beyond anything, the body will follow your directions. It only knows what you tell it. I'm sure right now you're probably asking, "Hey Vaishāli, why does it do that? Doesn't the body know I don't want to get sick?"

There is actually a great spiritual reason behind this. The body is designed to support our development as conscious beings. The body is here to act as a neutral form of feedback constantly reflecting back to us what we are doing with our attention - whether we are choosing fear or love. Dr. Norman Cousins, author of the groundbreaking book "Anatomy of an Illness" wrote about how he cured himself of a potentially terminal tissue disease by forcing himself to watch comedic movies and laugh for at least an hour a day. Now it does not take a brain surgeon to know that you cannot be laughing at the Marx Brothers and be choosing fear at the same time. Film producer Samuel Goldwyn was famous for his "Goldwynisms" and he had a few very humorous slants on health, such as: "If I could drop dead right now, I'd be the happiest man alive," "A hospital is no place to be sick" and one just about everyone can relate to, "I have been laid up with intentional flu." W.C. Fields had a physically-liberating emotional take on health care as well: "Don't worry about your heart, it will last as long as you live." Mel Brooks covered all bases, giving his body the ultimate instructions with: "Humor is just another defense against the Universe." James Thurber most likely explained why humor and laughter is perhaps the greatest panacea when he said, "Humor is emotional chaos remembered in tranquility." And as Groucho Marx said about my latest book, "From the moment I picked your book up until I laid it down,

I was convulsed with laughter. Someday I intend reading it." Laughter and willingness to move forward go hand in hand, and when you give that your attention the body will be under the impression that is what you want.

Wouldn't it be wonderful if we lived in a world where we ultimately found that the cure for the common cold is to laugh and love our way through the day? Just imagine Adam Sandler and Russell Brand receiving a Nobel Peace Prize for the latest advancements in health and medicine. Instead of an MRI, you got "The Family Guy". Just think… watching reruns of "Seinfeld" might be the perfect antidote for fear spread by watching the evening news. Health insurance companies would have to change their questionnaires to "Do you get your news from CNN or South Park?" Medical exams would go from "Turn you head and cough" to "Tilt your head back and laugh".

That was a good one! Ok, so where was I? Oh, yes! Going back to the Eastern self-healing systems defining the root cause of all illness as the direct result of the emotional responses created by what we give our attention to. The *Reader's Digest* indeed had it right all these years: laughter really *is* the best medicine. Laughter is positive, because laughter is always choosing love over fear. Laughter sends a message that life is good, and we are here for the sheer enjoyment of just being alive. When we laugh our bodies are under the impression that is what we want. So the next time you pick up a newspaper forecasting the end of the world… yet again, or your favorite news program wants to pass along its gift of a media-induced frenetic fear frenzy, remember your body is waiting, listening to see what you want… fear or love.

What do you have to lose if you choose to inoculate yourself with love and laughter? What does it cost you to let the body know fear is not a power you choose to recognize? Then, in the name of better health and a vibrant immune system, go to a comedy club, rent your favorite laugh-out-loud movie, read James Thurber or Mark Twain. Let there be no mistaking that enjoying life, resiliency to toxic situations and a positive outlook is what you want to learn from. See ya in the funny papers!

Ayurveda 101

*A*yurveda, the Eastern Indian system of self-healing, is translated as "the science of daily life." In other words there is an actual science to the understanding and execution of one's daily routine that is designed to promote balance and overall wellbeing.

The system is based on three doshas - three specific types of energy configurations that comprise all of life in the physical world. Since all of the information in Ayurveda is in Sanskrit, a sacred Indian language, the terms require an English translation. The three doshas are: Vata, which is air and space; Pitta, which is fire and water; and Kapha, which is earth and water. Let's take these one at a time.

Vata
Although air and space sound like the same thing, they are really very different. Space signifies an emptiness and air is what fills up the space. Vata governs the nervous system. Without it nothing would move in your body. Vata is the only dosha that moves. It makes your eyes blink, your blood flow and it is responsible for all those interesting and sometimes humorous (embarrassing) bodily noises. Vata primary people are small boned, prone to dry hair, dry skin and constipation. They are also creative, fast thinkers and talkers and occasionally a bit spacey.

Pitta

This dosha is fire and water, but this water is more like digestive juices, blood and bile. Pitta people are lean, athletic, competitive types and perfectionists. They are prone to infections, loose stools and burning disorders like ulcers and heavy bleeding. They are also very smart and quick minded; they like things done their way and organized to their liking.

Kapha

Kapha primary people are voluptuous like Marilyn Monroe and Angelina Jolie. All the classic beauties are Kapha primary. They have a tendency to put on weight if they do not work out and eat sensibly. Kapha crave sweet and creamy which can be their downfall. They tend towards congestive disorders such as excess fluid in the lungs and body, impacted lymph tissue and oily skin. They are the most compassionate and easy going of the three doshas. They also have the most physical stamina.

Every person is made up of a unique combination of all three of these energies. As a matter of fact anything that is living be it animal, vegetable or mineral is made up of these three energies. From an Ayurvedic viewpoint life is defined as these three energies coming together and death is when these three energies fall apart. It is essential to know what energy is your primary constitutional element, as well as your secondary and tertiary elements. Also important, in order to maintain optimal health and longevity, is to know your proclivity for imbalance.

The focus of Ayurveda is about achieving balance. This is accomplished by knowing what opposite energies to apply to your life and when to apply them. For example, Vata people crave dry crunchy things like salads made with cold, rough, raw vegetables.

Because the Vata element is cool and dry, people who are Vata primary tend to run on the cold side and have a low digestive fire, making these salads tough to digest. Vata primary people are best served eating warm liquidly things like stews and soups or things with plenty of oil (ghee). Vata primary people are already too cold and dry; they need to apply warm and hydrating energies to balance themselves both physically and emotionally. In Ayurvedic terms, once the body goes out of balance, the emotions and mind are going to be affected as well. Vata people like forms of exercise, such as jumping and running, that will provoke the Vata element. Instead, swimming in warm water or doing slow exercises that build core strength would best serve them.

There is a law in Ayurveda called "like unto like." It means that you will be attracted to energies similar or related to your predominate energy. For a Pitta person that means engaging in competitive or judgmental events. Pitta people like to be better than others. Pitta primary people make great engineers because of their fiery, cut through the problem oriented minds. Pitta people are perfectionists. They hold themselves to a high standard… and everyone else as well. Pitta people usually like alcohol and salty, spicy, hot foods. They want that martini or wine with fish, red meat, carrots, beets, tomatoes and diary products. For balance, what they need are the raw cold salads the Vata people are eating, with little or no meat/diary products. Their best forms of exercise are slowing down, yoga, using the balance ball or swimming… minus the competition. Taking a shot glass of aloe vera gel 2-3 times, spread throughout the day, is a Pitta person's best friend.

Kapha folks, oh, how they love their sleep. They enjoy being at rest and letting everything physically engaging take a back seat. Kapha primary people hate exercise and despise diets. Their motto is, "Salads are for rabbits." They crave ice cream, cookies, cake, potato chips, fried foods and fast foods. They prefer to kick back and watch the Vata and Pitta people run around and get everything done that needs to get done because life is too short. What a Kapha primary person really needs to stay fit and healthy is to get up before 6am and start the day with some kind of aerobics, getting sweaty and getting the heart pumping. They should eat only citrus fruit or berries for breakfast. They need to keep moving, with not too much sitting, and not too many carbohydrates; like Pitta they are best served avoiding animal products as well. They need to avoid sweets and take those salads away from the Vata people. Oil is the enemy of any Kapha person; they already have too much: excess water weight and oily skin.

Ayurveda is not for the faint of heart or for those deeply invested in denial about their shortcomings and self-sabotaging habits. It takes dedication, perseverance and a willingness to change what you are most comfortable with. Knowledge brings power. Ayurveda is all about taking your power back - balancing your energy by knowing what will resolve your present energetic health issues and offering you a greater path for personal growth and happiness. Conscious living is not always convenient living, but it is always the most beneficial life-sustaining course of action.

One Size Does Not Fit All

*N*ext to the notions that one can achieve a body without cellulite and a life without suffering, the greatest mistaken belief is that there is one diet, one type of oil, one form of exercise, one hormone supplement, one mantra or prayer, one rigid organizational life structure or one medication that will work for everyone. Most of us grew up with the "magic bullet" concept that science was going to invent this one universal panacea that would solve our problems throughout all of time. If you operate from the Western mechanistic paradigm, which dictates that every person is basically no different from any machine, like your car, then this idea makes sense. Everybody has a heart, two lungs, kidneys, a brain and a digestive system; therefore all bodies are the same. However, the Eastern systems of self-healing - Indian Ayurveda, Tibetan Ayurveda and Traditional Chinese Medicine - see human life as a completely different construct. They operate from an energy paradigm and view every person as a Universe unto themselves; each one completely different.

The Eastern philosophy makes perfect sense for anyone who has ever noticed that no matter what you may do or ingest in your physical body, what works for one person may not work equally for another. Yes, your mileage may vary. (That's why a three-minute commercial for a prescription drug has two and a half minutes describing the side effects – because not everyone has the same reaction.) Most heavyset people have noticed that their thin friends can eat the same thing, or even a greater portion, and still not gain an ounce. Skinny people may have witnessed that no matter how many weights they lift, they still never get the muscular definition their larger-boned counterparts get after putting in half the effort and workout time. Others still may have become aware of the fact that one herb or medication that eliminated a family member's illness had no impact on their own health dilemma. There are groups of people who feel healthier following a vegan diet. Some societies eat high fat diets including meat and live long lives with no adverse effects. This is not a conundrum; there is a good reason for all of the above.

The viewpoint of the Western medical system is quantitative. Its primary focus is on measurement: how much, how many, what size. All people are considered analogous. Height or weight will determine the medical action taken. Aside from that, if it works on one, according to allopathic medicine, it will be of service to all. Insurance programs also reflect this "one size fits all" medical approach in their policy construction and coverage of treatments.

Conversely, the Eastern perspective is qualitative. Quantity is not relevant. Eastern systems know that just because the packaging details, like number of organs or extremities, may be indistinguishable, that does not imply that the quality of energy making up each and every person's constitution or medical issue is the same. We are more than just the sum of our "parts."

The Eastern system perceives everything through the filter of energy. What is each person's energetic makeup? Just as no two snowflakes are the same, every individual is a manifestation of the unique signature energy frequency that holds their body together. These Eastern time-honored systems, which by the way have been around for thousands and thousands of years, take into consideration the wide differences in energetic characteristics. Some people have a bigger and heavier bone structure than their slimmer, less dense counterparts. Others have faster neurological responses and respiration. Some people can eat virtually anything, while others have an extremely delicate digestive system. Certain people are aggressive, hyper, motivated and competitive; some are calm, easy going and carefree.

These energetic differences are broken down into "body types" or "doshic constitutions" as discussed in "Ayurveda 101": Vata (air and space), Pitta (fire and water) and Kapha (Earth and water). All of us - people, cats, dogs, plants, insects, anything that is living, including the Earth itself - are comprised of all three of these energy elements, or we would not be alive

According to the Eastern healing sciences, the action of these energies coming together is the definition of physical life, and the disintegration of these energies is the definition of physical death. Furthermore everything that is living has its own organizational makeup and balance of each of these distinct energies. So, although one living being may have more Vata than Pitta, or more Kapha than Vata, everyone still has all three energy elements or they would not be alive.

Each dosha has positive and negative aspects. Each provides an element needed to sustain overall life. But, there is no one energy that is better or worse than another. For example Vata, because it is air and space, governs all movement. Without Vata our eyes would not blink, our heart would not beat and our blood would not flow. Without Pitta there would be no physical, emotional or psychological digestion. The energy of Kapha allows for bone structure, muscular development and a sheath to protect the nervous system. The downfall of a physical body is an element that is out of balance. Any single energy can go out of balance, or all three can go out of balance. An out of balance Vata is responsible for wasting away diseases like Alzheimer's or senility. Too much Pitta will create infections and blood disorders. Excess Kapha can form a tumor or cyst. All three out of balance is cancer. Furthermore, one element may show up primarily physiologically, while for another person that same element may manifest itself as predominately psychological. For the purposes of our sharing here, we are going to distill each element and not combine them as they normally appear in life, so that the distinctions in each doshic element can be better examined and understood.

Most Americans have a Pitta or fire primary body type. The classic fire body tends to be a lean, wiry body type that has a tendency to run warm. They can be aggressive or competitive and like things done a certain way. Pitta primary people make good engineers as they possess a strong mental fire, which allows them to organize concise thoughts, be attentive to details and cut or burn through what is unnecessary. If the person is Caucasian then they frequently will have a fair complexion and can sunburn easily. Our digestive system is governed by the fire element. So, if the Pitta energy is balanced, a fire primary person will have a good strong digestive system. They may even notice they get warmer after eating as their internal fire is rising to combust the ingested foods. Pitta primary people can have a predilection for loose stools, oily hair and skin and strong body odor. Emotions associated with an aggravated Pitta element are anger, jealousy, judgmental or critical, impatience, easily irritated and defensive. More balanced fire emotions would be reflected as a wise, thoughtful, fair and conscientious individual.

Vata body types normally have small, delicate body frames due to the large amounts of air and space that make up their constitution. Vata is also the wild card of the energy elements: it can manifest as an abnormally large or small stature. Conan O'Brien, the late night talk show host, is an interesting combination of Vata and Pitta. The fire element is evident in his red hair, a very fair complexion and a lean body frame. The Vata element making up his body shows up in his extraordinary tall, long and lanky frame with limbs that fly around as if he were in a perpetual tornado. Conan, like most Pitta primary people, possesses a quick, penetrating mind and a wiry body type. However his irregular, statuesque height is a classic Vata trait, since irregularity is a fingerprint of the Vata dosha. This is the reason Vata primary women are prone to irregular menstrual cycles. Other Vata primary or Vata imbalance symptoms include irregular appetite, irregular sleep patterns and irregular bowel movements, most likely constipation, but it can also swing back and forth between loose stools and constipation. Most Vata primary individuals are dealing with dry skin and dry hair. A Vata primary body type provides very little insulation between the skin and the nervous system, as the primary element is air and space. This means a Vata primary person, more than any other body type, is likely to suffer more traumas when involved in a mishap. Now wouldn't that bit of information be helpful in dealing with insurance companies when it comes to assessing how badly injured someone was after a car accident? Out of balance Vata-influenced emotions will appear as worry, fear and being high strung. When balanced, Vata emotions are playful, light hearted and extremely creative.

The Kapha element is energetically about Earth and water. People who are Kapha primary usually have a larger bone structure. Like Earth and water, Kapha body types have a tendency to hold on to energy. They are prone to gaining weight easier than either Vata or Pitta body types. However, when people with a predominate Kapha dosha do work out and eat well, they will develop a large, well-defined muscular structure. The Incredible Hulk comic book character is the perfect example of a strong, ripped Kapha body type. The Kapha body type has a tendency to live the longest. Like the competition between the tortoise and the hare, a Kapha primary person may start out slower, speak slower, take a longer time in organizing their thoughts and words, but in the end they have the accumulated energy of endurance on their side. Most Kapha primary people have thick hair, big eyes and lovely facial features. All classic beauties are either Kapha primary or secondary. As mentioned before Angelina Jolie and Marilyn Monroe are the perfect examples of Kapha beauties. Because the Kapha element holds on to energy, it is in the best interest of a Kapha primary person to get up by 6am and get in a workout right away. A Kapha primary body will start to gain more weight every minute they sleep in past 6am. Working out gets that sluggish energy into motion and initiates the fat burning mode instead of energy accumulation and weight gain. Getting up and engaging directly into motion are more Vata and Pitta friendly activities. The last thing an Earth body type wants to do is get up early and work out; they tend to be your typical couch potato. Kapha excessive emotions are anxiety, depression, feelings of isolation and heaviness. When Kapha-related emotions are balanced, they are compassionate, understanding, sensitive and patient.

These descriptions are an extremely brief introduction to these profoundly complex concepts. Of course everyone will see some aspect of themselves in every description, as we all are comprised of all three doshic energies to vastly varying degrees. The basic idea is that each body type is energetically, qualitatively different from the others: Vata people are prone to being dry, Kapha people will gain weight easily, and Pitta imbalances are the underlying cause of inflammation and ulcers. The bottom line is that there is never going to be one pill, one diet, one exercise routine that works for every body. Some bodies need cooling, others need warming; some require adding lubrication, while still others benefit from drying out. There is no pharmaceutical Holy Grail that everybody can take resulting in a miracle cure. There is no cookie cutter health program that will universally accommodate the energetic needs of every person, anywhere, at any time.

Understanding your energetic body type and determining your proclivity for imbalance are absolutely essential for organizing a hands-on personal health management routine. This is the first step in knowing what will or will not work for you. Individually and collectively we would all benefit from maturing beyond the concept that we live in a "one size fits all" world. The solution to our health issues and life management dilemmas lies in the wise understanding of what energies are coming together and forming our personal and individual human experience. The longer and more deeply invested we become in finding that one "magic bullet," the further we stray into ignorance of how to heal and maintain balance in our lives. After all, a robust and consistently healthy quality of life is the desire of every living person. The Western approach to wellness is not going to work for every person. If you are fortunate enough to have found a therapy that is working for you, you have accidentally stumbled upon an energy match for your issue. If you are like so many others that have not found a solution inside your cultural paradigm, may I suggest looking outside your culture? The idea that we are energy and not mechanisms is not a new or original idea. Modern physics is verifying and proving this to be the case with greater conviction and clarity every day. It simply makes enlightened sense to wisely respond directly to the energies that are contributing to and holding together your human experience of life.

Consciousness: What You Don't Know Might Kill You

*E*ver ask yourself, "Where does consciousness come from?" Or, "Can consciousness come from an absence of consciousness?" Albeit, not the subject of your everyday discourse, these are still interesting and relevant questions. When inquiring about consciousness a valid qualifying question might be, "What type of consciousness are we talking about?" For example, dreaming consciousness comes from the REM cycle. A medical coma consciousness comes from pharmaceutical drugs. Enlightenment consciousness comes from meditation or some other practiced ability to observe and focus attention. However, when it comes to your physical consciousness, such as how emotionally and mentally astute you are and how healthy you are on a cellular level, the answer might surprise you.

The Eastern sciences, such as Indian or Tibetan Ayurveda and Chinese Medicine, have a very clear cut and direct answer to this last aspect of consciousness. These ancient sources of wisdom say that the food you eat is the foundation upon which your emotional, mental and physical well-being is based upon. Ayurveda has a very succinct term for the physical body. It is referred to as the "Food Sheath." They call the physical body that because it requires a myriad of different types of food. It requires oxygen food, light food, physical "tactile" food, hydrating water food and solid alimentary food, all as sources of nourishment. The "Food Sheath" term eliminates all the "judgment" issues from the physical - no charges about the butt being too big or small; no painful comparisons or emphasis on beauty of any kind. The body is simply the "Food Sheath."

The physical body or "Food Sheath" receives its quality of intelligence from the food you eat. We're not talking brain science or rocket surgery here. If you start your morning by drinking nothing but coffee and eating a donut, then you run around all day, some time in the afternoon you are going to start tanking. You will find it increasingly difficult to focus and concentrate. You will find yourself becoming more and more agitated and impatient when life's daily dose of obstacles smacks you right on your... food sheath. You may experience shaking of the extremities or a headache. You may find your mind easily distracted and unable to remember simple details: where are my glasses, keys or cell phone?

As stated in age-old philosophy and co-opted by the high tech world, "garbage in; garbage out". That's because a calorie is not a calorie. The quality of your energy comes directly from the quality of the food/fuel you take in. Now Ayurveda goes deeper with this understanding than may initially seem self-evident. For example, if you eat a lot of foods that have been grown to produce no seeds, such as some types of oranges or watermelon, over time, that could compromise your body's fertility. After all what are seeds? They are highly concentrated forms of fertility consciousness/energy. Bear in mind these types of food would have to be pervasive in your diet and you would have to be exposed to these fertility-sterilized forms of foods consistently for prolonged periods of time. It is unlikely anyone is going to eat that much seedless fruits with no diversity. But what if all crop seeds were sterile? Would that change the dynamics?

With that in mind, let's now look at a pervasive form of food that we have all been exposed to for a prolonged period of time: GMOs (Genetically modified food organisms). Even though GMOs are foods that have been genetically injected with extremely poisonous material, the FDA in its infinite wisdom has declared that these foods do not require any testing whatsoever. In fact, the FDA has never done any testing on them! Monsanto has been legally, genetically poisoning our food supply for decades. It's no surprise that wildlife such as migrating birds will not touch a single kernel of GMO corn when growing side by side a crop of non-GMO corn. In fact no animal, other than humans, when given a choice, will consume a GMO food.

These animals intuitively know what Ayurveda and Chinese Medicine teach: food is your first wave of either medicine or poison. When you eat foods that are packed with Chi (life force energy), your mind, body and emotions are energized. When you eat foods that are packed with antioxidants, your immune system becomes stronger and empowered to destroy free radicals, because that is where the consciousness that directs the body comes from. Conversely, when you eat foods that have been genetically altered to contain chemicals that are designed to kill and destroy life, how can that have a positive affect on your energy?

In addition to the GMO nightmare, Monsanto has produced "terminator seeds." These are seeds especially designed to die after one crop. They carry a sterilized energy that does not allow another generation of plants to grow. Why? Money. The farmer has to go back to Monsanto each and every growing season for more seeds, so Monsanto's profits have increased accordingly. It is pure and simple greed, even though the planet destroying consequences of this greed are neither pure nor simple.

How can Monsanto get away with poisoning our food supply? You may find it interesting to know that many high-level FDA people are former Monsanto employees. And, that's right; you guessed it. Incestuously many of the upper level Monsanto employees are former FDA staff. Well, maybe it isn't interesting. Pathetic may be closer to the truth. We have the best politicians money can buy.

Most people are unaware of these healing sciences that have survived scrutiny for thousand of years. What they have to say about the quality of consciousness that feeds your health or disease is still relevant in today's world. You need to look no further than cancers, both common and exotic, which are on the rise, or that the rate of obesity and insulin resistant disorders like diabetes have been increasing exponentially. Attention deficit disorders and autism cases seem omnipresent. Isn't it interesting that the expansion of all of these diseases happens to magically correspond to the ever-increasing presence of GMO's in the American diet.

If you are thinking, "Oh, but I'm not eating GMOs," think again. You probably are; you just don't know it. Since the FDA has declared that foods containing GMOs do not have to be labeled as such, you are not informed that the food you are consuming is toxic. If you are not eating organic foods exclusively, if you are eating or drinking anything with high fructose corn syrup (sodas, ketchup, fruit juices), corn, soybeans, cottonseed, sugar beets, canola oil, most fast food meals or pre-packaged processed foods from large food corporations, you are most likely eating GMOs. For more information please visit: http://www.nongmoshoppingguide.com/tips-for-avoiding-gmos.html.

What you may have become painfully aware of is that you are fatigued all the time. You may have noticed that you having a harder time concentrating or remembering things. You may have observed an increase in health issues or poor sleep. You may have sensed that the consciousness of the body is off in some way but have not yet connected all the dots. All of these are profound reasons to examine what you are consuming that is feeding the quality of consciousness that governs your human experience.

Socrates once commented, "The unexamined life is not worth living." If he were alive today, his consciousness cry might be, "The unexamined diet is not worth eating."

Five Alternative Healing Tips for a Healthy Lymphatic System

*I*f it isn't the swine flu, then it is the bird flu. Or some other illness the media is heralding as the next big pandemic. The truth is no one wants to get sick or feel bad. No one wants to place his or her job in jeopardy, missing productive days due to illness. If you are self-employed, you know all too well if you don't work you don't get paid. So what ongoing reasonable actions can we take to intelligently build and maintain a healthy defense against illness? What is the best way we can ensure that the body is strong enough to overcome any potential health hazard it may be exposed to? The answer is to protect, strengthen and support the immune system, the body's first wave of defense in the prevention of illness, whether contagious or media inspired.

The lymphatic system, to a great degree, governs the body's immune system. Unlike blood, lymph is a whitish-colored fluid that only moves in a one-way direction throughout the body. This system filters out viruses, bacteria, and even cancer cells before they can re-enter the blood stream. The tonsils, thymus gland, spleen and nodes are all part of the lymph organ system. Keeping the digestive and lymphatic system healthy is the cornerstone to every person's well-being.

5 Simple Tips to Support the Lymph System:

- *Avoid ingesting iced beverages and foods straight from the refrigerator.* The greatest sea of lymphatic tissue is in the digestive system. The body functions best at a temperature of 98.6 degrees. Healthy lymph feels like oily water and is pumped throughout the body primarily by the skeletal muscles. It needs this warm environment to remain in a healthy fluid-like state. When you eat or drink cold foods and liquids, it stuns the lymph system causing the oily water lymph to congeal into a more jello-like consistency impeding its free flowing movement throughout the body.

- *Watch your intake of herbal supplements.* There have been many time-honored herbal formulas that enhance lymphatic function such as echinacea, goldenseal, red root, red clover, licorice root and astragalus root. Often times these herbs help by stripping away a layer of debris from the lymph system's filtering operation, but in the process they can dry out or deplete this system. Therefore they work best if not taken over long periods of time. Most recommendations are 7-10 days.

- *Try Chi Nei Tsang.* Lymphatic drainage massage specifically targets the lymph system. It aids in the breaking up of congestion within the lymph system, tones and supports the lymph nodes as well as facilitates the fluid's movement throughout the body. Chi Nei Tsang massage works directly on the entire digestive system and is a powerful technique for lymphatic care. More importantly Chi Nei Tsang is designed to be self-administered, so once you learn how to do it, you have a lifetime of free treatments, and best of all, no insurance forms or bureaucratic companies to deal with. For more information go to: www.chineitsang.com

- *Treat the body to the T-Tapp exercise program.* Since the lymph is pumped throughout the body by the movement of skeletal muscles, the correct exercise that maximizes this effect is critical. There are many exercises that provide some lymphatic support, like swimming and aerobics. However, if you want to maximize your efforts, the most effective method is a widely acclaimed program called T-Tapp. The T-Tapp exercise program is designed to drain the lymph system as well as balance hormones, burn fat and build the muscular structure from the core outwards. Best of all T-Tapp requires no equipment… just your body, which means you can do it anywhere and no ongoing fees. Walking is also great for the lymph system and there is also a T-Tapp method of walking that increases those benefits dramatically. The T-Tapp motto is work smarter not harder. So why not do the same for your lymphatic system? For more information go to www.T-Tapp.com

- *Cold laser treatments* boost the lymphatic system, support drainage and keep the fluid moving. Cold laser sessions are completely painless and often-times yield immediate results of their positive benefits. Cold laser sessions offer a safe treatment option for the very old or very young or those already weakened by drugs or chronic illness. Acupuncturists, chiropractors and other alternative health practitioners may offer cold laser treatments in conjunction with their regular health care packages. There are even cold laser treatment centers.

A Few Little Things

*B*eneficial information does not always have to come in pre-tentious, pontificating packaging. Sometimes learning just a few simple tips for more conscious living can make the most useful and positive changes in our lives. To that end, listed below are thirteen understated yet profound tips for improving the quality of one's health as well as assisting in that perennial task of getting an edge up on anti-aging and weight management.

1. Walking after you eat. Walking is actually a very powerful digestive aid. The Eastern Indian system of self-healing, Ayurveda, advocates for "the journey of a 1,000 steps" after consuming food. The walk doesn't have to be long; it just needs to be embarked upon after mealtime. So if you have a dog, take your fur-covered friend for a once around the block. Your pet will be grateful and it will serve as a post-digestive gift to yourself. If you can't walk, massaging the feet relaxes the body and strengthens the digestive system. There are many reflexology points on the foot that connect with our internal organs, thus bringing immediate benefit and support.

2. Waking up at 6 am and exercising gets you the best return for your workout investment. This is especially helpful if you are large framed and prone to gaining weight easily. In Ayurveda, different times of the day have different qualities of energy. For most corpulent people, getting up early in the morning is absolutely the hardest most unpleasant task of the day because the energy influence of 6-10 am has a heavy, sedentary quality. According to Ayurvedic philosophy, overweight people will actually gain more weight the longer they sleep in past 6 am, as this is when their metabolism is the most sluggish and energy conserving.

Getting up at 6 am and working out counterbalances that natural slowing down, lethargic, weight gaining tendency. It puts one's metabolism in fat burning mode rather than fat accumulation mode. If you are going to bite the bullet and work out routinely, getting up early and starting it first thing is the smartest way to maximize your benefits.

3. The body likes a temperature of 98.6 degrees, because the organs in the body function best at this temperature. As a matter of fact the body can even function well hotter than that, like when we get an infection and the body turns up the heat. But it does not like to get colder. Eating or drinking cold food and liquids stuns the organs by forcing them to run colder than they are designed to function. Think of the stomach as a pot that sits on your stove. You want there to be a consistent flame under that pot so that everything you put into it gets cooked thoroughly.

Refrigerators and ice machines are fairly new advents in the history of humankind. Our bodies have not historically evolved into ingesting cold foods and liquids. In addition to adverse effects on organ function, there are emotional repercussions from internalized lower temperatures as well. Ingesting cold cuisine shocks the stomach and spleen/pancreas, which in turn creates an emotional backlash of worry and anxiety. The habit of eating cold foods and drinking iced beverages may be behind your waking up at 4 am worrying about various issues in your life.

Another point to consider is that when the internal organs get colder, that will cause a slowing down of the digestive system and its calorie burning efficiency, thus increasing weight gain from whatever is consumed. Consuming cold food and beverages literally freezes weight in the body, stunts the digestive system and promotes the release of cold-related emotions such as stress and worry. Drinking warm liquids and avoiding cold foods will assist you in gaining less weight as well as processing and releasing toxic emotions. So, before you have that ice cream sundae or root beer float, think about making sure you also have a hot beverage that you sip frequently to give your body a chance to warm up and recover from overwhelming the internal organs by lowering their preferred inner temperature.

4. Food combining is a topic that gets very little attention. Most people will go out of their way to buy and prepare an organic and nutritious meal. But if the foods are combined incorrectly the internal results can be disastrously unhealthy. There are many food-combining rules that can be refined indefinitely and endlessly, making them too rigid and hard to follow. For the sake of simplicity we will focus on some elementary points.

Do not combine fruits with grains, meats or vegetables. Fruits are mostly water and take about an hour to digest. Grains, meats and vegetable matter takes about three times longer. So when fruits are combined with these slower digesting foods, they will putrefy within the digestive tract. This means that even if you eat organic cereal with organic milk, and throw on some organic fruit, the whole thing will become a toxic mess in the body.

Fruits have their own food-combining rules as well. Citrus fruits should not be combined with non-citrus fruits. Melons and strawberries should be eaten by themselves and never mixed with anything else. That means that strawberries and bananas may taste great together, but your body will not benefit from the combination. Melons and strawberries go in the "eat them alone or leave them alone" category.

Ayurveda calls mangoes the "Queen of fruits," and mangoes are immune to the rule of fruit combining. According to Ayurveda the mango is the only fruit that can be combined with other foods and not become toxic. So enjoy that mango lassie with a guilt-free conscious.

Ayurveda calls asparagus the "King of Vegetables" and says if you are going to eat only one veggie make it asparagus. It is a deeply detoxifying and nutrient enriched food. Asparagus is a pricy vegetable, but if you treat food as medicine, this is one dish well worth considering.

The bottom line when in doubt about food combining: eating a kosher diet will always ensure the healthiest dietary combinations. (A kosher diet follows Ayurveda food combining.)

5. Eating root vegetables heals, supports and sustains the root chakra. All root vegetables such as carrots, turnips, beets, radishes, etc. are medicine for the body's root chakra energy system. The root chakra is an energy center located on the pelvic floor. It is all about supporting life and survival on the most basic of levels. Especially during times of extreme stress, when the body is under pressure, think of root vegetables as your first wave of medicine for the root chakra.

6. Laughing before eating relaxes and opens the gall bladder duct. Eating during a sales meeting, while emotionally upset or in the company of people you do not like or trust will cause the gall bladder duct to constrict and narrow.

When stressed or emotionally compromised this tiny duct between the liver and the gall bladder can be the first part of the digestive system to contract and the last to relax. If you have a history of gall bladder challenges, laughing and lightening up can be your best digestive aid.

7. Everyone wants better posture, but forcing that result by tightening the back muscles is not the best way to achieve that goal. A more efficient way to achieve better posture is to lift up from the sternum, which expands the chest naturally, instead of tightening the back muscles. Then turn the thumbs outwards and back when you stand or walk. This will gently rotate the shoulders back and correct slouched posture without over correcting.

8. Ayurveda suggests that any organ that is exposed to the air needs oiling on a daily basis. Edgar Cayce also agrees with Ayurveda in the suggestion that there is value in placing a few drops of organic castor oil in each eye just before going to bed. By the time you wake up the body will have completely absorbed the oil and your vision will be clear and refreshed. Beyond lubrication, another advantage to castor oil in the eyes is that it supports the liver. According to the Eastern systems of self-healing, the eyes are connected to the liver. When the body is forming in the uterus the eyes and liver develop at the same time from similar tissue. When the liver is ill, such as with some forms of hepatitis, the eyes will become a discolored yellow. So whether or not the eyes are windows to the Soul, they are definitely a window to the health of the liver. When we stare into a computer or television screen for long periods of time or spend too much time in the sun, the eyes can overheat the liver energetically. Castor oil, when applied externally, is energetically cooling and will literally pull the excess heat out of the liver and the eyes. When castor oil is taken internally it is heating. That is why taking a spoonful or two of castor oil will inspire a bodily waste evacuation.

There is an Ayurvedic oil especially designed for the nose. It is called "Nasya" oil. This oil is to be used in the morning and evening. One lays on a bed or floor with the nostrils pointing upwards. Then 5-7 drops are placed in each nostril and inhaled deeply, driving the oil back up into the nasal cavity. In addition to lubricating the nasal passageways, inhaling this oil does wonders for clearing up allergies to animal fur and various forms of pollen. It also helps to ease shoulder and neck tension and stress.

There are several types of oil specifically for the hair, scalp and detoxifying the brain. Brahmi and Bhringaraj are the most popular. Ayurveda describes the head as actually having a type of energetic vent system. These oils enter the vents and lubricate not only the hair shaft and scalp but also the brain itself. These oils can be used individually or in a formula of half and half that can be mixed and combined to get the full spectrum of oilation benefits.

Ayurveda suggests that the movement of life itself is drying to the body. Since the skin is the body's largest organ and has the most exposure to the elements, oiling the body head to toe before showering is recommended as one of the top three daily routines for a long and healthy life. Once in the shower do not soap the oil off. Allow the water to drive the oil deeper into the skin, and then towel dry as normal. The body is designed to clean itself from the inside out. Using the typical soap and water shower protocol will dry the top layer of the skin which compromises the body's natural cleaning from the inside out. Oiling the skin supports the body in cleansing itself from the deeper tissues outwards.

The type of oil that one would use would depend on the body type of the person in question and their proclivity for imbalance. Almond oil is one of the few oils that can be used by nearly every person, although for best results, one should consult an Ayurvedic practitioner for an exact determination.

9. Getting to bed between 9:00 pm and 9:30 pm will provide a better quality of sleep. Our bodies go through natural cycles daily and nightly. The body is designed to begin to slow down at night in preparation for sleep. This why it is best to stop eating after 7pm, as the digestive system is slowing down as well. When going to bed with enough time to drift off to sleep before 10pm the body will be primed for the best recuperative rest. After 10 pm the fire in the mind will start to rise and become more active. If you are awake and doing things, you will most likely experience that second wind and find yourself possessed by the need to just get that perennial "one more thing" done. Needless to say, as most people have already noticed from personal experience, the more active the mind, the more difficult it is to fall asleep.

10. Menstruation wisdom. This tip is just for women. Avoid a strenuous workout the first 3 to 4 days of your menstrual cycle. The menstruation process is one of the more profound ways the female body detoxifies. Working out is all about building the body up; detoxing is about supporting the body in releasing.

These are widely divergent activities. When you exercise during the menstrual cycle you are telling the body to both build up and let go. Energetically this is very confusing to the body's natural intelligence.

The energy flow of the body changes during menstruation. Bleeding, from an Eastern perspective, is a fire event, and fire naturally rises. This upwards energy flow is not ideal during the menstrual cycle. The body naturally shifts the energy to flow downwards for this localized fire event. When a woman engages in any activity that brings the body's energy attention upwards, it is in direct conflict with the body's natural downward shift of energy flow during menstruation.

This downward energy movement is designed to help purge the toxic blood down, out and away from the body. Women prone to endometriosis need to be especially carefully in preserving this natural downward energy flow and not confuse the body by directing energy upwards. Endometriosis, from the Eastern perspective, is caused by the fire energy flowing back upwards, instead of flowing downwards during the menstrual cycle, thus taking the endometrial tissue with it.

This means even avoiding the upwardly inhaling the nasal oil in addition to any energy work done around the head. Also avoid bodywork such as deep tissue massage or Rolfing above the waist. Foot reflexology and bodywork downwards along the legs is fine, since it will encourage a downward movement of energy.

11. A tongue scraper is a simple and low cost health feature everyone needs to keep with their toothbrush. At night while we sleep one of the many things the body is doing involves detoxification. All of the body's internal organs are connected to the tongue. This is why Ayurvedic and Chinese Medicine practitioners ask to see the tongue. From examining the shape, color, pits, dents or other topical features, a good alternative health practitioner can discern a great deal of information about the overall health of the body.

In the morning after waking up the best way to start the day before eating and drinking is to use the tongue scraper. Start as far back as is comfortable and bring the tongue scraper forward. All the discolored materials that are scraped off the tongue are toxins the body has taken the time during the night to bring up through the internal organs and push out through the tongue. Using a tongue scraper is also a very effective way to make changes in your diet, by seeing directly the next morning what your body is discarding on the tongue as toxic and non-useable. The tongue can be lightly scraped until the residue is no longer appearing on the scraper. Usually this is about 10 times. Then clean the tongue scraper as you would your toothbrush.

12. Swishing sesame oil in the mouth for ten minutes will enhance dental hygiene. Statistically India is the country with the highest number of diagnosed cases of diabetes. Yet it has the lowest cases of dental decay. Swishing organic sesame oil in the mouth for ten minutes has been a time-honored way of improving oral health. This can be done while watching television, reading, washing dishes or any activity that does not also involve talking. This only needs to be done once a day, and is best to do before bed, as it will also help keep the mouth from drying out while sleeping. A dry mouth will encourage the growth of bacteria. The magic number is ten full minutes and then spit the oil out. Do not swallow.

13. CCF tea is the ultimate beverage for a long and healthy life. Take equal amounts of organic cumin, coriander and fennel seeds. Boil for 3-5 minutes, then strain out the seeds. According to Ayurveda this tea formula has long been valued as the best tonic for what ails you. The combination of seeds is a great digestive aid as well as internally cleansing. There is a saying in Ayurveda that nothing bad can happen to you if drink enough CCF tea. Freshly sliced ginger can also be added and boiled with the seeds to add a fire balancing digestive quality. The tea by itself is slightly bland so honey and lemon can also be added to make the taste more interesting.

Summary: When making changes in your diet and lifestyle it is also best to start out with what is easy and simple. Making changes gradually is the best way to ensure that you can incorporate beneficial habits routinely as well as keep your life balanced by not overwhelming yourself with too many changes too quickly.

Also remember that food is your first wave of medicine. When you are grocery shopping for yourself and family, if what you are throwing into your shopping cart is not useful as medicine to the body, don't buy it.

These tips are designed to be a simple, quick and easy way to bring some profound improvements to the quality of your life with the least amount of effort. Remember, radiant health and a balanced lifestyle start and build on itself with every conscious choice you make.

Mirror Mirror on the Wall

Body Image Repair

I have taught many classes over the years on various aspects of life- management. I usually start by asking what issues people are struggling with the most. That is what I focus on. What I have noticed is that a greater number of people are requesting help in the area of how to deal with suffering. Self-inflicted suffering they experience at their own hands: how they perceive their own body image. For many women, and an increasing number of men, feelings on this subject range from mild emotional discomfort to outright self-hatred every time they look in the mirror.

Being a female in 21st century America, and being in my fifties, I can honestly say in the spirit of "been there, done that" that there is nothing I fail to understand about hacking oneself to pieces with an overly critical eye. I suspect every female, over the age of twelve, knows from personal experience something about this painfully slippery slope where self-identification and self-worth become grotesquely morphed together into one irreconcilable mess.

You can blame the media all you like with those beautiful, thin supermodels on television and in print ads, but the real underlying problem starts from within. Seeing who you really are through the filter of body image is like trying to get a clear picture of yourself in a fun house mirror. The lens itself is bent and twisted rendering everything in its reflection an easily misconstrued version of reality. Like all other issues that originate with perspective, the problem is a symptom of an inner distortion: a bigger picture misunderstanding where truth has gotten overshadowed and lost along the way.

The most essential pattern that needs to be addressed is that we think we are our bodies. We take bad hair days personally. We see body weight as an all out war we wage on a daily basis. We imagine we look unattractive in almost everything we try on. The old saying, "We have seen the enemy and it is us" has never been more appropriate. We intellectually understand that we are not the physical trappings of this world, but we don't *live* it. We know on some level that we are not our bank accounts, yet when there is not much money in the checkbook, our self-esteem and self-confidence gets as low as the dollar figure. So it is no surprise that the physical packaging, what we carry with us everywhere we go, gets the same or a heightened sense of myopic self-absorbed, misplaced self-identification. After all, what is more "in your face" than your face? And what is more "up close and personal" than the body you experience yourself inhabiting?

The classic Eastern forms of self-healing and philosophy, such as Buddhism and Taoism, remind us that we are not our bodies. We *have* a body, but what we really are is *beyond* the body. We are a form of consciousness, a form of Spiritual wisdom and intelligence that existed before we came here to the planet Earth and took a body, and will continue to exist long after we have discarded this modus operandi and moved on to our next evolutionary step. According to these time-honored traditions, the body is actually a separate intelligence, a separate form of life. It is not our essence, which is consciousness itself.

That is why I refer to the body as "the" body and not "my" body. The challenge lies in the fact that our awareness has a very intimate relationship with the body. So we are intimately aware of what the body is experiencing and feeling: hunger, exhaustion, excitement, overweight, pain, etc. And it is this quality of mind/body overlapping intimacy that can make lucidly perceiving the boundaries between real self and corporal self nearly impossible to distinguish.

However, from this pinnacle vantage point of Eastern philosophical wisdom, a liberating healing truth emerges: we are not the body. Our value, power and worth are a non-competing, totally separate, imperishable and unfading reality. Vedantic psychology asks us to remember that we existed before this present packaging, and we will continue to exist after it. So how do we start to segregate who and what we really are from the anchor of the physicality we embody?

To explore this more authentically you have to step way back to allow yourself the opportunity to glimpse a more comprehensive, honest landscape... the Big Picture. A few more steps; you're not back far enough yet. Okay, that's better. Now you're ready. The body ages - you do not. The body gains weight - you do not. The body experiences illness and disease - you do not. You are timeless and immortal consciousness itself. The body takes on and goes through all these limiting states for you. Why? Because the body is offering you an embodied education in personal growth by taking on everything the physical world can throw at it.

Knowing that the truth shall set you free, here are the keys these ancient systems of self-knowing advise you to incorporate to release the perpetual perceptual chains that bind you. The body willingly agrees to this one-sided relationship unconditionally. The body agrees to go through aging, illness, injury, birth defects, surgeries, cellulite and unfashionable hair cuts because the body *loves* you that much! Shocking isn't it. Just take a moment and let that sink in. How many people do you know that would unconditionally agree to grow old for you? Gain weight for you? Lose hair for you? Be crushed in car accidents or be blown to pieces for you? The body is the greatest, unconditional life-long love affair you will ever have.

Reflect for a moment, if you will, on all that your body has agreed to take on and go through for you - without hesitation and without compensation. A lifetime of constantly changing challenges and susceptibility to unspeakable vulnerability and suffering. Now consider for a moment how you view the body. What do you tell the body? Do you have a relationship of gratitude and support for the body? Or are you incessantly spewing an inner narrative of toxic venom accusing it of "unacceptable" and "unlovable" behavior?

Imagine there was a person standing next to you your whole life. And this other person shoulders all the health consequences, all the hormonal transformations, organ transplants, bad boob jobs and hair replacements. This other person carries the burden of all the poor choices you make: excess weight from lack of exercise, health issues due to fast food. Would you treat this other person the way you do your body, violently screaming that they are an idiot, stupid, unlovable, uncooperative, ugly and repulsive? Or would you be cheering them on with loving words of gratitude, support and encouragement for their selfless devotion to your evolution?

I can answer that from personal experience. I have lived with incredible physical pain at times for years at a stretch. What helped me to heal was to thank my body for taking this process on for me. I became the body's best cheerleader by always reminding it that it had the wisdom and ability to recover from anything, and I loved it with all my heart. I discovered that when I acknowledged the body for its unconditional love, I was able to move through the pain without being crushed by it. I was able to focus on the health results I wanted without taking the difficulty of the journey so personally that it crippled me.

Whether or not you embrace what Buddhism, Taoism or Vedantic philosophies have to say about the human experience, here is the bottom line: pay attention to how you feel when you engage in an abusive rant, accusing your body of ruining your life and making you miserable. Is this the relationship with the body and mind you want to continually invest in? When has criticizing and despising the body ever solved a single body image problem? Has it made them all worse? Would you be indifferent to other people treating you in this way? Of course not. So why do you tolerate your own unjust behavior when you have the power to stop it? Look around at your friends and loved ones. Would you practice unleashing that kind of cruel hostility on the most irreplaceable relationships in you life?

What if self-loathing was a choice, and you could make a different choice by shifting what you give your attention to? What if your body thrived on being your greatest love affair? What if the body required your patience and loving kindness to correct medical problems? What if the body was desperately in need of compassion and understanding in order to release the weight it feels heaped upon it and relentlessly burdened with? All of this begs the question: what kind of relationship can your body rely on you to provide? The next time you slip back into the habit of looking at the body with disgust in your heart, remember that any relationship that lacks love and compassion is destined to failure. You have the power to transform this relationship into the greatest love affair you will ever know. It starts with learning how to love and respect your way to success, because if a lack of self-acceptance and resentment were going to solve your problems... it would have by now.

Spirit

The Answer to the Meaning of Life is... Multiple Choice!

*R*eality: this crazy little thing called existence. What is it? Most likely, Lilly Tomlin gave the best celebrity answer in her one-woman show. She described it as little more than a collective hunch. Of course, she also described reality as a crutch for people who can't cope with drugs and a leading cause of stress. And here I thought it was something complicated. Start with a collective hunch, throw in some drugs, and add a dash of stress. I got it! Reality is college life in the 1970s!

For the sake of this discussion, it is not important whether or not we fully comprehend or even agree upon the scientifically approved definition of reality. The mechanics of reality, quantum or otherwise, are immaterial. What *is* paramount is the meaning and perspective we freely give to reality. From a purely existentialist point of view, reality is an indestructible freedom - a freedom of choice. You are free to choose your attitude, perspective and the meaning of your life's situations, challenges and relationships. The entire content of your life is completely predicated upon the imbued meaning you freely choose to give it. It is a daunting task; so much is riding on your choice. A choice most of us are not even aware we are making, much less have so much invested in.

The definitive expert on the meaning of life is Victor Frankl, author of the classic, *Man's Search For Meaning*. In his book, Frankl even goes so far as to say that choosing the meaning of reality is a pre-requisite for good mental health. He states that therapy and living an "examined" life can help us grow beyond our baggage and inner wounds. However, without choosing life-sustaining meanings, our minds will never heal or be completely whole. Great! More pressure. Now if you make a foolish choice you put your relationship with quality mental health in a precarious position. I guess that explains why so many of us have "issues."

Three existential philosophers from Texas, ZZ Top, ask the practical question, "How could anyone be so unkind as to arrest a man for driving while blind?" Their subtle point is to consider how much of the time you are even consciously aware of the navigating choices you make that drive your life. How deliberately conscious are you of the meaning you attribute to the events of your life or even of the world in which you live? I suspect that most of us are so distracted and caught up in the movement of our everyday existence that taking the time to choose the meaning of our life's lessons as they unfold and present themselves simply gets overlooked.

So what choices are worth making and what choices are not worth making? After all, if the quality of our human growth and our perceived value, power and worth are a direct by-product of the meaning we freely choose, then the prime objective of a successful life would be to consciously make wise choices.

First let's consider what happens if we decide not to make a choice – that is a choice that is not worth making by the way. How many times do you see senseless acts of violence on the news or witness an insensitive act by someone? The usual thought response is, "I could have lived without this inconvenient occurrence in my life." When we fail to harvest meaning from the events in life, we plant the seeds of being powerless, a victim, worthless, miserable and unhappy. Meaning provides the distinctly human ability to cultivate depth of character and gives us access to the strength to grow beyond any limitation.

To illustrate this, a man came to Frankl completely distraught by the death of his wife. She had died a few years earlier but the man just could not get over her death. Frankl asked the man what would have happened if he had died first instead of his wife. The man answered that his wife would be struggling to move forward, as he was now. Frankl suggested the meaning behind the man's suffering was that he was going through it so his wife did not have to. The man then responded, "Okay. Now I can move forward knowing I am doing this for her." Nothing in the man's life actually changed *except* he now had a meaning for his suffering, which made it bearable and provided him with a means to evolve beyond the stagnation of grief.

There are an incalculable number of things in life that we cannot control or change. Without applying meaning, we have the accumulation of pain and suffering without a means of transcending it. If no attempt is made to find meaning, then what we have in fact chosen is an absence of meaning in our personal experience of reality. Welcome to the void. Whenever we create a "quality meaning" vacuum in life, the emotional and psychological aspects of our existence start to erode and diminish. Ultimately this will affect the physical. As Frankl points out, the ability to choose meaning in our lives is what makes us distinctly and uniquely human. So whether we derive life-enhancing meaning or suffer from a lack thereof, our choice is going to affect every aspect of our reality.

Nature does not like a vacuum. When we fail to bring a transcendent meaning to our lives, whatever stimulus we are exposed to moves in and defines our internal understanding and knowing of ourselves. The risk is that without actively participating in the search for meaning, the "know thyself" quest becomes a shallow, unsatisfying excursion.

Frankl based his theory of the critical nature of the search for meaning on his real life experience as a holocaust survivor. But what most interested me in this search is this: within the framework of personal and individual freedom to create meaning, are there some universal choices that would bring liberating results no matter what the underlining circumstances might be? If you are struggling with the loss of a loved one, employment layoff, divorce, foreclosure, medical complications, bad hair day or all of the above is there a choice you could make, a default, which would bring life-enhancing meaning to your experience unconditionally? And if so, what exactly is that meaning choice? We always ask why bad things happen to good people, but what I'm asking is what do good people choose when bad things happen?

Although not on the scale that Frankl went through in a Nazi concentration camp, I found myself searching for meaning amid the grief and sadness following four deaths within the span of two weeks. Two were violent and traumatic deaths; two involved watching the final suffering of loved ones as they crossed over. I wanted to choose a meaningful way of growing beyond the shock and unhappiness. I wanted to choose a deliberate and conscious method of life operation. What could I choose to bring alive and nurture an intelligence that would counterbalance the outflow of life that had just occurred? Is there a meaningful choice I could make that would cover this deep and widening gap, providing a stable supportive path for moving forward through the tragedies and ugliness that find their way to this planet?

I needed to know where the truth that sets one free could be found. So I started in the most fundamental area of life ~ relationships. I wanted to search for meaning in the human contact I encountered with every person, no matter how brief. These passings had awakened the realization that tomorrow is promised to no one, and that with each interaction we have with our fellow human beings, any one of them could be our last. I wanted to choose to connect with everyone I encountered with the essence of the old Christian adage, "love thy neighbor." I wanted to know if this, the greatest of all Spiritual Laws, was a choice that would bring meaning to my life, ubiquitously, no matter what the source of limitation might be. If I died unexpectedly, and the last person I spoke to was a hi-tech customer service rep in India, I wanted to choose that even as transient as that contact might be, not counting my time on hold, I was going to speak to this person with the same integrity, patience and understanding that I would to the most important person in my life. That was the meaning of reality I chose to bring to that exchange. I found that honestly thanking them for being of service brought a profoundly comforting meaning to my life. I also tried to make them laugh if I could.

Interjecting a quality of basic human kindness into all relationships I encountered was the meaning I choose to see in the loss I could not change in my own life. My choice, love, considered to be the highest ethical philosophical teaching, and laughter, did in fact bring a life-liberating meaning regardless of the source of the suffering. The old Christian adage "love thy neighbor" worked! It worked to provide that universal, one size fits all meaning. I could apply it anywhere and everywhere in my life and it brought a transforming power that gave my life a richness of meaning and purpose.

Don't get me wrong, I still cried and grieved for those loved ones who died. Emotionally digesting these events still manifested to its fullest extent and intensity. Finding meaning did not give me a vacation from being human; it is not a reprieve from working through challenging emotions. It did not change the details of the exterior world. However, infusing this search and alignment with meaning made it a journey I could endure with grace and dignity. A quality of self-realized development strengthened my understanding of what is truly valuable and important in life and what it means to be fully human.

The extent of my wisdom is this: meaning is chosen by your free will. It is not inherent. There is no "meaning instruction tag" sewn into the fabric of life. Finding a meaning choice is not based on how much money you have or don't have. It is not determined by what education you have or have not completed. It has nothing to do with politics, religion or sexual orientation. It is an internal action that is applied externally through the exercise of free will.

So much of the suffering on this planet is intrinsic to the human experience itself. Regardless of what your life is yielding, you are not alone. Many others on this rock know what it is like to share your pain. If the "love thy neighbor" choice achieved such a deep-seated across the board deliverance quality of meaning for me, I suspect there is boundless value in it for you as well. After all, my suffering and your suffering do not exist in a vacuum. We are all connected.

When I choose to interact from a core of love, I can see the Divine in all and it endows my life with a pristinely elegant, expansive, tangible sense of meaning. The best part of all, I have yet to find a downside to relating to others from an authentic inner place of tolerance and compassion. And most importantly remember, when a customer service rep asks you if there is anything else they can do, always answer with, "How about a life without suffering and a body without cellulite?" And when you find one… call me day or night!

What's Your God's Name?

*V*edic, Buddhist and Taoist forms of psychology offer radically different perspectives on things most of us in the West take for granted. For example, your chosen relationship with God. Most Western-minded people think of God as the creator of the Universe, as the focal point of worship and reverence, as final judge and emancipator. Also from the Western mindset is an understanding that each person has a personal relationship with God. However it is on this exact point where Eastern psychologies break from the traditional viewpoint with a completely different twist. God, from a Vedic, Buddhist or Taoist practical stance, is inseparable from what you give your attention to. In other words whatever you habitually focus on, whatever gets the bulk of your attention, is what you have just made your God.

This means that if you are thinking about that next cigarette all the time, you have made that pack of twenty your God. If you keep thinking all day long about sex, money or when you are going to get that next well-deserved martini, then you have just made those things your God. It's a rather shocking way of looking at life and what we hold as Divine, isn't it?

Modern life holds some extra special complications that did not exist, or were not even imagined, at the time of the Buddha, or when Lao Tzu was penning the Tao Te Ching. In those ancient times there where no cell phones, no tweeting, no Internet, no texting, no X Box or television reality shows. Hmm… suddenly the concept of what is your God is becoming stickier and more convoluted than ever before. When you're in your car and the cell phone suddenly started ringing, does your attention shift from keeping your eyes upon the road and your hands upon the wheel to answering that beckoning cellular song, like Ulysses caught in the grasp of the singing Sirens? If so, guess what? Your worship service has just started; you are bowing down at the altar of electronic technology.

How much of your day do you text, surf online, play video games? What is your most loyal relationship as far as what gets your attention? If you consider for a moment the implication of whatever you give the focus of your awareness to, you have just made your God, you may either want to release a primordial scream or immediately convert to another "religion." This notion if nothing else takes existentialism to completely new and diz-zying heights.

Let's kick this up a notch, shall we? How much of your attention is consumed with thoughts of worry? How many times does your attention circle around the gravitational pull of the notion that you do not have enough time and money? How many ways do you imagine life conspiring to go out of its way to let you down or disappoint you? How many times do you ask yourself, "What else can go wrong?" My, my, my, can it be that the average person makes lack, loneliness, victimhood and unhappiness their God ever so consistently and fervently? If nothing else you can see where an atheist in this scenario might feel like they have the last laugh - a "Get Out of Jail Free" card when it comes to self-examination.

And self-examination is really the point here isn't it? To ask yourself whether or not what you are giving your attention to is possessing you. Are you in an imprisoned relationship of indentured servitude to what you invest the bulk of your energetic obedience and awareness to? Can you live without your Blackberry or iPhone? What would the quality of your life be like if you took a week or month-long timeout from Face Book? Is what you are giving your undivided attention to setting you free?

The question of whether or not there is a God, and if there is one, what is the nature God, is not going to be resolved here. This Eastern perspective of what each of us makes our God is designed to provoke self-examination and thoughtfulness, not mind numbing, pedantic, controlling doctrine. It is not about proving or denying the existence of God or defining Divine characteristics. It is about knowing with deliberate conscious choice what you construct your life and value system around. It is about asking yourself if what you are infusing and investing with life-giving attention is really the most important thing or relationship in your existence. If the answer is no, then it begs the question what is, and where is it in the awareness priority list of your life?

What you gain when you ask yourself, "What am I making my God in this moment?" is the honest ability to reconcile what is in your heart with what is on your mind, and what actions you take as a result. It makes you accountable for feeling deeply the consequences of what you consider important in your life, while destroying your ingrained habit of going through life on autopilot. This perspective makes it more challenging to look back on your life and ask yourself, "Where did my life go?"

The most refreshing element about the Eastern view on what we make our God is that it takes all the established, well-defended dogmas and theological theories and throws them out the window. It is the great equalizer on a practical level of what you are living right now in this moment. Do you have the same God as Charlie Sheen, Homer Simpson (mmmmm… donuts) or Gandhi? Do you worship at the same altar as Victor Frankl or Donald Trump or Oscar Wilde? You decide in the privacy of your own mind. No need for a vow of poverty or celibacy. Circumcision, baptism and confession are all optional. What is required is that you show up fully for your life and ask yourself on a moment-to-moment basis, what are you plugging your life force into? What are you giving your power, attention and energy away to? On a lighter note the more convenient aspect of this Eastern perspective is that conversion is as easily and simply done as changing your awareness, your point of focus. So choose wisely.

What We Cannot Hear Enough

*W*henever I share the life and wisdom of Emanuel Swedenborg (1688-1772) with my radio show listeners, the people who read my books and magazine articles or with those who attend my many classes and lectures, I always start out by introducing him as "my boyfriend." That introduction accomplishes a couple things.

First and foremost, it makes an 18th century scientist/mystic more approachable to a 21st century audience. In our current paradigm, scientists can't relate to mystics, and mystics don't relate well to scientists. How could he be both? Through a technique of controlled breathing, Swedenborg could enter a state of concentrated focus. This trance-like state enabled him to literally master every known science in his life and later gave him access to the Angelic community. This is a difficult concept for most people to grasp, so who would not feel slightly alienated by that? Who would not be intimidated by a man Stanford University voted the most brilliant person to have ever lived on the planet!? Swedenborg left us with an enormous canon of scientific work. Merely reading these volumes would be a daunting undertaking. Not to mention his achievements as a profound mystic discoursing with people who had died, with Angels and with... well let's just say beings we would not call Angels. When you add in the over four and half million words he wrote about the nature of the Spiritual Worlds, how they are organized and why we, as Spiritual beings, benefit from having a human experience, you do not exactly have a man the average person feels they can immediately relate to on a personal level. As you can see, a definite overachiever.

The second thing that introduction does is bring the context of his writings down to a level uncomplicated and relevant to one's everyday life. The heart and soul of his wisdom is, after all, about examining what we are doing with our attention. Let's face it, there is nothing more germane to everyday life than what are we are choosing to give our attention to and thereby what we tell ourselves inwardly as we move through our day.

Now let's start with the Swedenborg basics. Most people find it absolutely astonishing to discover that Swedenborg defines our Divinity as inseparable from our attention. The idea being that our awareness and our Spiritual Identity as Divine Love and Wisdom are in fact one and the same. I have to massage into my audiences' psyches Swedenborg's perspective that we do not have Divine Love and Wisdom. It is not a possession; it is not a matter of being deserving or worthy enough. We *are* Divine Love and Wisdom right now, just the way we presently are, and the way that Spiritual reality manifests in the physical word is as consciousness itself. Once people understand that their awareness *is* Love, so whatever they are giving their attention to, they are also giving their Love to, we can move on to the next vital piece of information.

There are core ideas that run throughout the thirty some volumes of Swedenborg's work that describe the Spiritual Realms: how what we give our attention to in our everyday human experience instantly affects our Spiritual evolution. I find that these dominant core ideas create an internal infrastructure for the deepest most empowered "know thyself" investigation possible. In laying the groundwork for this inner "know thyself" path, people cannot hear, read or give enough of their attention to these liberating, self-empowering cores ideas. Swedenborg articulates a Truth that sets us free. How often do we need to set ourselves free? How many seconds, minutes, hours are in a lifetime? And it is so easy to forget them or allow the material world to eclipse them, that we just cannot hear these core ideas enough.

All of Swedenborg's writings centralize on a single Law that all of the physical and non-physical worlds revolve around. That Law is: *you are what you love and you love whatever you give your attention to*. This Law permeates every aspect of life: psychological, emotional, physiological, relationships, financial and Spiritual. Even after you die, according to Swedenborg, you are still subject to this Law. So remembering it throughout your day is unconditionally paramount. What it breaks down to on a practical level is this:

- Look at what you are giving your attention to

- Be aware of how it makes you feel.

- If you are focusing on something that makes you feel limited, stop!

- Put it down and re-focus on something that is unlimited in nature.

When you give your attention to what is limited, you love living a hellishly limited existence. When you give your attention to what is unlimited, you love living in an unlimited realm. Why? Because of this Law: *you are what you love and you love whatever you give your attention to*.

When we examine this Law from the viewpoint of what limited things you might be giving your attention to, the answer is most likely all too familiar: "I don't have enough time." "I don't have enough money." "Why does everything in life have to be so hard?" "Everyone else has someone to love them and is happy except me." "Why is it that I never get the winning lottery ticket, but some worthless idiot who is probably going to spend it all on cars and drugs in the next three weeks always does!?" The reason all these limited things we could potentially give our attention to come so easily to us, is because we loyally practice focusing on "the limited" so frequently. It has become a habit.

Now let's explore what is unlimited that we could be giving our attention and therefore our Love to. For nearly all, this is also the most unfamiliar. It just so happens that the unlimited Truths that set us free are also the same core ideas running throughout Swedenborg's writings. The principal and most important one is to remember your true nature and to separate your attention from toxic self-defined illusions. This means seeing, relating, identifying and speaking to yourself as Divine Love and Wisdom and nothing less. It is understanding that you, as Divine Love and Wisdom, are the most powerful force in the Universe:

- You have more power than any challenge you are presently going through.

- Everything that touches your life is working for you because everything serves the most powerful force in the Universe: Divine Love and Wisdom.

- As the most powerful force in the Universe you can only create learning experiences that work for your highest good, no matter what it may look or feel like. Furthermore, you do not have the power to create those self-expanding learning experiences before or after you needed them.

- You have free will. You determine what gets your attention… what you want to love. You choose if you want to sign up to learn more about limitation or unconditional Love and abundance. You are not a victim or without power.

- You are treasured and adored. Speak to yourself that way. Treat yourself that way. Feed, care for, be patient and love yourself with that quality of integrity.

In order to align your attention with these unlimited things you must be willing to grow beyond the concept, the self-identified restriction, that you "do not have enough." You must be willing to no longer see yourself as the person who is a day late and a dollar short. You must be willing to see whatever touches your life, be it an overdue bill, an I.R.S. audit, a medical diagnosis, or the loss of a relationship or job as providing your life with the seeds of a greater growth. In order to be in right relationship with these unlimited ideas you must also be willing to take your power back from the outer world. You must be willing to no longer allow your value, power and worth to be determined by how much money you have, what kind of car you drive, how much weight you have gained, what level of education you have received, what your marital status is or what job level you have achieved. These things no longer have the ability to define you.

You must exclusively know that your value, power and worth is that you *are* Divine Love and Wisdom, and no one and no thing has the power to change that.

Another primary idea Swedenborg explains is that all suffering has a single point of origin. The genesis occurs whenever you think, define or relate to yourself as something less than Divine Love and Wisdom. When that happens you put a rippled energy wave of misery into motion. There is only one possible result that can come from loving something untruthful about yourself ~ and that is unhappiness. This transpires when you tell yourself that you are not good enough, you don't measure up and you will never get it right. Who has not experienced first hand the reductionist quality of life that ensues when you give your attention to things like: "Why am I so stupid?" "Can't I ever do anything right?" "I am so unlovable." "I don't deserve better." "I will never amount to anything."

When Swedenborg was alive many people came to him and asked him to contact loved ones who had died, taking sensitive information to their graves with them. He was tested hundreds if not thousands of times. Every time he gave an answer he was proven to be 100% accurate. Many people witnessed these events and wrote about them. These first-hand recorded accounts became known as Swedenborg's "minor miracles." Just to cite a few of the well documented things that he shared:

- Who would be the next one in a room to die?

- His own day and time of death.

- The exact day and hour a sailing ship would arrive from an ocean voyage.

- He was able to describe events happening hundreds or thousands of miles away from his physical location long before mass communication.

All these things astounded the people of his time, and the people who read about them now. Only Swedenborg did not write a single word about them himself. Certainly the man had the time, energy and means to have written about these things in great detail, but he chose not to give it his love. Why? Because he did not feel they were important.

What he did feel was of critical importance was to write over thirty volumes and over four and half million words about this Law: *you are what you love and you love whatever you give your attention to*. He did spend the last 27 years of his life emphasizing the supreme importance of taking your Love back from any and all limitation, aligning your inner dialogue and self-perception with the reality that you are Divine Love and Wisdom and realizing there is no pay off, unequivocally nothing in it for you to identify with anything else.

When people asked Swedenborg, "How do you do that? How do you focus on what sets you free and nothing else?" He had two pieces of advice. The first is whenever you find yourself giving your attention to things that take your life to a limited place, stop. Put it down and focus on the truth of who and what you are. The second bit of advice was what he called "forgetting and remembering." Remember to give your attention to what takes your life to an unlimited place and simply forget everything else. Or as I like to say it, "How do you get to live unconditionally in an unlimited place? The same way you get to Carnegie Hall... practice, practice."

If you have something more worthwhile to do with your Love than transform all limitation into unlimited Truth that sets you free, you have my undivided attention.

Are You Full Of It?...
Divine Love, That Is

*W*hen is lying not lying? Is it when you have nothing to lose by being honest? Does it depend on what "is" is? Maybe it's, "No officer, I really only had two beers." Or could it be one of those harmless little personal miscommunications, like when you answer your wife's perennial question, "Does this outfit make my butt look big?" Possibly it is when you are throwing that bag of Oreo double-stuff cookies and Ben & Jerry's ice cream into your shopping cart, telling yourself that you're going to make this last the rest of the month. Or is that next pack of cigarettes always the last one you are ever going to buy? Maybe it's when you are filling in your expenses on that extended 1040 form because, hey, for all they know, that lunch at the strip club was a business meeting. That one doesn't even pass the smell test.

A lie is not a lie only when we tell ourselves something and believe it *is* the truth. Surprisingly, the most damaging lie we never recognize as being bogus has nothing to do with our finances, body image, diet or lifestyle. Buddhism would call all of these things impermanent in nature. They come and go; they create a constant state of flux and change. It is understandable that we should be subject to distraction when involved with things that are forever permeable. I mean who, at one time or another, has not been taken in by a shell game? It is challenging to know where the pea is when it is zipping around, continuously in motion. But we are not talking about being taken in by sleight of hand here.

Without question, the greatest prevarication has to do with our eternal and unchanging nature. It's ironic that the one aspect of us, which always has been and always will be, is the very thing we have the most difficult time honestly acknowledging. Not only is the truth about our genuine nature the single biggest lie we tell ourselves but it is also the most lifelong, systemic lie we buy into with well-practiced consistency. How can this be? Let's examine how we infected our perception with this unrecognized fiction.

How many times during the course of your day do you tell yourself that you screwed up, that you are stupid, fat, undeserving, impoverished, helpless, powerless, under supported, overworked, not appreciated, destined to be lonely, unhappy, rejected, always in the slowest moving lane and, the most loathsome of them all, that you are unlovable? The eternal and unchanging fact about us is that we do not have Divine Love and Wisdom we *are* Divine Love and Wisdom. It is our true nature; we are inseparable from it. When you *are* Love, being deserving and worthy of it are no longer issues. When you *are* Love, it cannot be lost or stolen, misplaced or diminished. And the best news? You don't have to earn it. When you *are* Love, the most powerful force in the Universe, how can you also be a limited state of existence at the same time? Simple. You can't! It is a lie!

When the most pervasive fabrication in all of human history creeps into your life, how do you resolve it? By aligning yourself with the truth? When you worry, you are defining yourself as "less than" in some context. Do you settle that inner conflict by throwing fear at it...or your Divinity? When an inner narrative starts rambling off all your perceived flaws, how often do you silence that toxic voice with the truth about your real nature, that you do not have Love, you are it? When you are relating to other people, situations, or experiences, how often do you tell yourself there is only one power in this instance that you recognize and that is Divine Love and Wisdom? Do you advocate that as Divine Love you simply do not recognize the power of fear, intimidation, cellulite, divorce, bad hair days, obnoxious telemarketers, rude drivers and ill-fitting clothes? How often do you remind yourself that all of physical existence was created for the convenience of your Divine and Sacred growth? Everything in your life is designed to work for you because as Divine Love, you rock, you rule, you are the senior intelligence because you do not have Divine Love you **are** it - without exception, without conditions, without question, without apology.

The good news about this ugly, most disease-riddled lie we tell ourselves is that we can put it down. We can grow beyond its tyranny. We can recognize it for the trash it is and stop justifying its delusional presence as truth that has any real power in our lives. We can fully embody the truth of who and what we are. We are the ones who have diligently mastered the practice of buying into this dysfunctional negativity about ourselves; we are the ones who now have the ability to claim that we have learned everything we need to from that lie and will no longer feel its burden or give it our attention.

Imagine how free life would feel, living from a confident place of truth about yourself as a force of Divine Love right here, right now. You could now see yourself as above the anxiety and worry you had previously invested so much time in and focus on experiencing yourself as Divine Love. After all Divine Love neither relies on temporal matters nor perceives the temporal world as more powerful than itself. The higher truth is that we are all here to realize ourselves, and we cannot do that buying into the biggest most unacknowledged lie in the world: that we are somehow less than Divine Love itself.

Only we have the power to take our lives back from the lie we tell ourselves. What do you have to lose by replacing all the stories of "less than" with an open and honest acknowledgment of yourself as Divine Love? Well, let's see. Worry would get kicked to the curb, harsh criticisms and judgments would evaporate from the ether of your life, depression, unhappiness, discontent, disappointment and anxiety would all have to find a different zip code from your nervous system. It looks like all you have to lose is your loyalty to limited states of existence. I suspect you can afford that. What if you choose, as something new and exciting in your life, to replace that lie with an unwavering dedication to experiencing yourself as Divine Love, until you got as good at that as you are at lying to yourself now? Of all the things worth exploring, choosing and indulging in, I would say this would have to be pretty high on the personal achievement grocery list.

We really don't like it when other people lie to us but if we stopped lying to ourselves about our true nature, it would take the sting out of it when others did it. Once we make ourselves immune to the suffering that lying to ourselves about our Divinity inflicts upon us, the negatively charged thoughts or words aimed at us by misdirected personalities drop harmlessly to the ground without their poisonous sting. If enjoying a better quality of life within your skin is not sufficient motivation to curb the addiction to seeing yourself through the big lie filter, then maybe occupying a place where the world cannot rip you a new one is just the incentive you have been looking for. Either way, I know you will find that when it comes to wearing the truth about who and what you are, Divine Love and Wisdom are one size that fits all.

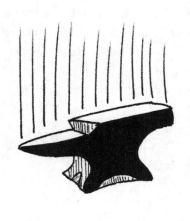

Celluloid Heroes

I have always had the greatest respect for cartoon characters due to the sheer force of their resiliency. Amazing is it not? What I would not give to be able to shrug off, without a second thought, the trauma of an anvil dropped on me from several stories high or possess the ability to bounce back after being shot in the face at point blank range with a shotgun, walking away with only slightly singed hair and a bewildered look on my face, leaving no permanent injury or scars. Imagine then how immune these toons must be to the cost of gasoline, the onslaught of monthly-incurred bills, constant price increases by the Acme Company (especially if you are a coyote) or the latest news broadcast of doom and gloom. Yes, right next to a body without cellulite and the ability to perform without Viagra, it seems cartoon-like resiliency would be the ultimate state of empowerment, balance, guaranteed happiness and insulated tranquility (unless, of course, you are a coyote).

Yet it seems that cartoon characters are blessed with this invincible quality because some human being *imagined* that quality into a frame-by-frame existence. So if Chuck Jones can do it, Walt Disney can do it and Tex Avery, the famous wild man of animation, can do it... why can't we? Does Wile E. Coyote possess greater powers than the average human being? Can Sponge Bob Square Pants really be more enlightened than you or I?

Why is it that we do not focus the lens of our perspective on the same mastery of resiliency that cartoon characters seem to have and by which they seem to mock our very existence?

The first reason would seem fairly self-evident... cartoon characters do not take themselves nearly as serious as we do. **"My stress, my anxiety!"** We proclaim it as if it was a Divinely guided Law that all beings should bow down before. Second, cartoon characters are not invested in defining themselves by their state of limitation. Porky Pig has never defined himself as a being a speech impediment. Yosemite Sam has never pigeonholed himself a rage-a-holic that has no value outside of anger management classes. It never occurred to Sleeping Beauty to limit herself to the label of the "ultimate narcoleptic, sleep dysfunctional Diva." Homer Simpson has never let his history of failure limit his ability to show up for each and every present moment anew. So why is it that we protoplasmic characters settle for an infinitely more inferior ownership and resiliency of self, value, power and worth?

Cartoon characters easily accept a new life script... something human beings are not always willing to do. Human beings love to cling to some past hurt or restricting memory of themselves, unwilling to embrace a new character storyline about their potential. Cartoon characters only live in the "now" - the present moment. Bugs Bunny shows up as if he had never been hurt before by past memories paralyzing his ability to visualize a greater outcome. (Even when he didn't take that left turn at Albuquerque and missed the Coachella Valley Carrot Festival.) Not once have I witnessed Fred Flintstone hold a grudge against Barney Rubble he could not get past. It seems we have so much to learn from these hand-drawn and computerized personalities.

What allows for this transcendent animated behavior is the capability of another fellow human being to be able to *imagine* it. This makes sense because all of the great Spiritual traditions say that if you cannot *imagine* you are senior to your everyday worries, you will never realize you are. If you cannot conceive the reality that you are Divine love and Wisdom, you will never see you are beyond your self-imposed stories of self-reductionism. If you cannot embrace a perspective of yourself as beyond the limitations you are here to grow beyond, you will never expand into that truth. If you cannot experience yourself as deserving and worthy of happiness and abundance, you will never manifest and align yourself with that potential.

Maybe cartoon characters are the most realized Spiritual teachers of the 21st Century. I draw comfort from that (every pun intended). I have yet to see a cartoon character that is immune to life's challenges and traumas, especially if you are a coyote. I don't know about you, but I prefer a role model that has had to pull themselves out of the same deep, ugly, painful trenches that I too have had to extricate myself from, minus the Technicolor embellishments.

What I most love about cartoon characters is their natural response to reality as a fluid and flexible state of being. I have yet to see any cartoon character ever take reality as seriously as the average human being does or to even claim that they know what reality is. I have also yet to see a cartoon character die from a heart attack, suffer from high blood pressure or find themselves caught up in a paralyzing addiction to CNN or the Home Shopping Network. I have yet to witness a cartoon character ask, "Does this make my butt look big?" Or have a bad hair day that ruined one second of their existence.

Cartoon characters, as in the tradition of any great Spiritual teacher, show us that resiliency and unconditional happiness are possible. They do not do this through dogma or emphatically defended doctrine. They do not try to scare us with threats of abandonment by God if we do not do it right. They have no "buy or die" belief systems. They do it by modeling that it is a choice. When faced with a choice between love or fear, cartoon characters will often explore the fear choice, just as we all do. But in the end they are the untarnished beacons shining forth the value of choosing love every time, unless, of course, you are a coyote.

Maybe that is why cartoon characters do not die. They have no regrets to lament over on their deathbeds. Toons are beyond the fear of a personal death; they know they cannot die. And the real interesting thing is that most of them do not need a near death experience to know that no matter what form they are in, their life in some manner continues without end. What would that kind of certainty be worth to the human race at large?

No human being is perfect, and some of us have more apparent flaws than others. So, while we still live in a world where televangelists mercilessly assault their viewers with fear-contaminated messages, where ministers are cheating on their wives, betraying their families, stealing money from their congregations, I am comforted and heartened to know that the cartoon Spiritual teachers of the world are eternally pristine from corruption. I know that Wile E. Coyote always pays his bill at the Acme Company. I know my favorite television show will never be interrupted to bring viewers a special broadcast, then cut to a news conference where Mickey Mouse, flanked by Minnie loyally at his side, has to explain why he was arrested in a cheap motel room with underage rodent prostitutes and a kilo of Colombian powdered "catnip" in his car. Yes, as long as people need to be reminded that they can grow beyond any limitation life throws their way, as long as people require a shining example of a life led by imagining oneself beyond the grasp of unhappiness and fear, I feel tremendously blessed to know that the best and finest Spiritual teachers are only as far away as the cartoon network. Without them, the Acme Company would surely be in Chapter 11 for selling defective products.

Kinetics Magazine
Interview With Vaishāli

1. Vaishāli is such a beautiful and unusual name. Please tell me the story behind it.

I studied Indian Ayurveda with Dr. V. Lad. According to this ancient system of self-healing, there is great value in changing your name at least once, if not more frequently, in one's lifetime. The idea is that each person holds a plethora of unresolved trauma in relation to their name. Think of all the times someone called your name and said, "Why are you so stupid?!" Reflect back on all the occasions when you were sitting in class and you thought to yourself, "Please, don't call on me, I don't know the answer..." and the teacher called out your name. Or whenever a bully called out your name just before they inflicted physical/emotional/social pain upon your life.

Changing your name allows you to grow beyond these limiting, self-defining moments. It gives you permission to expand your sense of self-identification. It nurtures a new beginning.

I felt it would be incredibly hypocritical of me to teach this philosophy and cling to my own myopic label. So I tried it. I changed not only my first name but dropped the middle and last names as well. I found it to be blessedly liberating and I highly encourage others to try it. Not from an intellectual viewpoint but rather from personal experiential knowledge.

2) **You're one of the most entertaining teachers on the spiritual circuit today! You've coined the name, Beyond Karma Queen and The Wild Woman. What inspired you to create this professional persona?**

I have found that a lot of people who teach or represent spiritual teachings were people I felt very uncomfortable identifying with. I did not see anyone who shared spiritually relevant information living a really fun, playful life. If I am going to give my attention to someone who claims to have the wisdom to improve my life, and they look, sound and feel boring, uptight, rigid, formal and confining... I am completely turned off.

For me enlightenment should translate into lightening up. In my mind, spiritual maturity is *not* allowing life to have a stranglehold or death grip on your experience of the present moment. So I wanted to break the mold and live the truth that each of us is unique and designed to celebrate our personal individuality - to model the truth that Heaven is expansive and large enough to embrace everything and everyone, even the most "out of the box" personalities.

3) **You are also known as the Purple Princess; why do you always wear the color purple?**

Since I was a child I have been absolutely fascinated by the color purple. Sometimes I will find myself staring at it, as if I have never seen it before.

However, when I was a child the fashion world did not really cater to this color. It has only been in the last 15-20 years that you could get almost anything in purple. And now that I am an adult and can buy whatever I want... I go passionately pervasively persistently purple.

According to the Hindu tradition, purple is Shiva's favorite color. Shiva is considered to be the most powerful of all the Gods because Shiva was willing to step forward and drink the world's poison, transforming it into unconditional love.

So, I see the color purple as representing the transformation of the worst, the most traumatizing of experiences into unconditional love.

4) Your childhood was greatly challenged by alcoholic parents and physical deformity. How did these early experiences help to shape your spiritual destiny?

We all come to the planet Earth to grow and evolve beyond any and all limitations. We all come here to learn how to identify with ourselves as Divine Love and absolutely nothing else. These childhood experiences simply highlighted what I had already agreed to focus my growth on before arriving here in a physical body.

These events underscored what my Spiritual identity desired to grow beyond. These limitations provided me with the Blessed opportunity to start creating a new response to suffering right from the gate.

These challenging situations also instilled a deep-seated understanding of what it means to extend and live a compassionate and accepting existence. To inspire me to live and let live, independent of intellectual judgment and criticism, without giving my power away.

5) In early adulthood, you were diagnosed with a terminal illness. Please share the details and how this devastating event forced you out of your cultural paradigm and ultimately to your healing.

I was raised just like everyone else in America. When you do not feel well, just go to your friendly local doctor, take a pill and make it all go away. Do not examine your life; do not consider your diet or lifestyle; and for God's sake, do not look at what you give your attention to.

I had been experiencing abdominal pain for well over a year, and it kept getting worse. When all else failed, my doctor suggested exploratory surgery. After the surgery, all my doctor could state with any clarity was that all the organs from the stomach to the rectum where in crisis. He took out a quarter and said, "The liver and small intestines are the worst. I could flip this coin to determine which organ will shut down first, the liver or the small intestines. I do not know why but that is most likely how you will die."

The good news is I was willing to accept that I needed to look beyond "better living through chemistry." I was open to exploring alternative perspectives and methods. All I knew was that traditional Western medicine was not "people friendly." It was not comprehensive enough to offer me anything practical, and it was not educating me on what options I might utilize. Little did I know at the time, this was a profound opportunity for growth in my life.

In my attempt to suppress, or at least manage some of the mind-bending pain I was in, I discovered the ancient Chinese internal organ massage called Chi Nei Tsang (www.chineitsang.com). This literally translates to transformation of the internal organs through Chi energy. This system taught me how to breathe in a manner that is detoxifying to the body and emotions, as well as providing me with an on-going practice on how pull old, stagnant, traumatizing charges from the body. From there I branched out and studied Indian and Tibetan Ayurvedic medicine, which showed me how to balance my body type through diet and lifestyle.

I write a great deal about this in "Wisdom Rising." Before this medical crisis I had been literally addicted to worry and fear. I had no idea that my thoughts, emotions, experiences and perceptions existed as a form of food ~ a non-physical form of food. I was ingesting this negativity but I was not letting any of it go! I learned that thoughts, emotions and experiences are here to enhance me and make me stronger and wiser. I slowly started to realize that these energy forms of food are here to serve me and that it is not useful to see these things as having more power than I do. It would be like sitting down to breakfast and seeing the bowl of corn flakes as having more power than I do. Not a good way to start the day or progress through life.

I awakened to the greater understanding that digestion is really a metaphor for life. How well are you digesting your life? How effectively do you realize that what does not serve you is the waste portion of your life and that it can be released now, versus how much of the painful and limited aspects of life do you hold on to because you do not see it is the waste portion of the program?

6) **A very serious accident almost took your life as well. Do you feel this was another necessary and spiritual wake-up call?**

There is an old saying, "The greater the student the greater the lesson." The car accident forced me to graduate from childish, inner limitation.

Before the car accident, I had been studying and practicing Ayurveda which means the science of everyday life. And there really is a science to the execution of everyday life that keeps us in balance. I knew what would promote healing and maintain a life-sustaining support system for my body type.

I had also been studying and practicing the Spiritual Law, "You are what you love, and you love whatever you give your attention to." I had been reading the teachings of the 18th century Swedish mystic Emanuel Swedenborg. He writes that we do not have Divine Love, we ARE Divine Love and our awareness and spiritual identity are inseparable. Therefore when I am giving something my attention, I am also giving it my love.

He states that as divine love we are senior to any and all limitations on the Earth. That, in fact, we are here to experience and identify with ourselves as Divine Love and absolutely nothing else, unconditionally. That means we come here to recognize only one power, and that is Divine Love and Wisdom.

When the accident occurred, I was still recognizing the power of fear, worry, intimidation, scarcity and abandonment. After the car accident if I wanted to survive, I had to be willing to grow beyond that life diminishing loyalty, the habit of giving my attention to those limiting, hellish thoughts. I had to be willing to give my love, my full, undivided attention, to the story that everything that was happening was working for me or it would not be allowed to touch my life. I had to do this to the exclusion of all other stories, no matter what the outer world threatened or looked like.

I had to take my power back from anything that did not acknowledge my divinity as Divine Love and Wisdom. I had to be senior to the physical pain I was in, the car accident trial, which by the way I lost. I had to grow beyond the ugly divorce I was also going through at the same time and the betrayal that relationship inflicted. I had to identify with infinite abundance when I could no longer work and lost my business and my life savings. I had to BE LOVE NOW, unconditionally.

7) With all the major life obstacles that have confronted you, how did you manage to keep such a sparkling sense of humor, and optimistic outlook on life?

At the end of the day, if you cannot laugh at all the pain and limitation, what is the point of life? I was not able to control the woman who hit me in the car accident. I was not able to make my now ex-husband behave in a more humane, honest manner. But what I could do and can control is what I give my attention to and my attitude about what life throws my way.

As Dannion Brinkley is so fond of saying, "In the Spiritual realm it is not what you do, but why you do it that matters." I know it is not what I do that liberates my Soul but why I give something my attention that matters. I may not be able to stop or censor what the world throws my way but I will always have the power to choose how I respond to it. And the bottom line is... humor and laughing simply makes me feel better than helplessness and bitterness.

My health may have suffered from time to time. My emotional process may have become occasionally overwhelmed through the years. Who hasn't been through that? However, for me, humor is my spiritual support and I was not going to permit laughing at this endless parade of suffering to become a collateral causality of life's slings and arrows of outrageous misfortunes.

8) **What advice would you give other women, in full maturity, regarding their magnificence and importance in a society that has a negative attitude towards aging?**

I see the process of aging as an opportunity to remember I am not my packaging. I existed before this body; I will exist after it. Everything in life is an invitation to identify with Divine Love exclusively in an arena in which I cannot fake it. You are what you love and you love whatever you give your attention to. You are a timeless and immortal force of Divine Love and Wisdom and no one and no thing can take that from you... unless you let it.

Society may have its issues with aging, but I get to choose what I will give my attention to and how I feel about it. And the truth is, the body ages. I do not. I am eternal, unchanging Divine Love. That is my story and I'm sticking to it!

9) **In my opinion, your first book, *You Are What You Love*, is a masterpiece and belongs on everyone's nightstand. It is so well written, incredibly enlightening and thoroughly delightful. Please explain the title and give us the book's three main messages.**

If I could have said it better than Emanuel Swedenborg, I would not have stolen these words directly from him. But then I only steal from the best. And honestly, there is no better way to wrap your mind around it than, "You are what you love, and you love whatever you give your attention to." That is and always will be #1.

#2 You do not have Divine Love; you ARE Divine Love. Love is not a possession. No one can take it from you. You do not have to prove you are deserving and worthy of something you already are! You do not have to wait for someone to throw you a few crumbs.

As Divine Love, you are also a form of God consciousness, for when was God ever separate from love? As Divine Love, you do not have value, power and worth; you are value, power and worth, for when was love and God ever separate from value, power and worth? You are Divine Love, God consciousness, value, power and worth and no one and no thing has the power to change that!

#3 As Divine Love... God consciousness, the most powerful force in the universe, you do not have the ability to create a learning experience you do not need. There are a lot of things God can do but create a learning experience of itself it did not need is not one of them. You can trust your life. You can trust what you are creating and when you are creating it as you do not have the ability to create a learning experience before or after you needed it. There is nothing about effectiveness and efficiency God consciousness fails to understand.

If you needed to be doing something else or living somewhere else in order to grow and learn more efficiently, you would be doing it already. As Divine Love you simply do not have the power to create learning experiences that do not serve you.

Rock on!

10) You say that we love whatever we give our attention to. So, do you advise that people simply overlook or ignore all the things in life that worry, concern or create fear within them?

I advise that people do not give their power away to worry and fear. I go into more detail on this in "You Are What You Love©." We are here to explore what it means to live a humanly and divinely balanced life. Give the temporal world its due: pay the taxes, balance the checkbook. But do not let the outer world overshadow your attention. Give the inner world its due as well. That means acknowledging the truth about yourself. You are not life's bitch. You are a force of Divine Love that no one and no thing can take from you. Everything that happens here exists for one reason only… it serves YOUR growth.

As Swedenborg phrases it, "We must live according to our love." What that means is this: when you give your attention to hellishly limited things like worry and fear, you spiritually live in a hellish place. When you give your attention to unlimited things, like the truth about your value, power and worth, you live in a heavenly, unlimited place.

No one can create a learning experience they do not need. If people need to learn there is nothing in it for them to respond to life with hellishly limited thoughts, then by all means continue to do that until you realize there is no payoff in it for you. As Jesus said, "When did worry ever add one inch to your stature or one day to your life?" As Mad Magazine's Alfred E. Newman said, "What Me Worry?" (You find spiritualism in the most unlikely places.)

All I'm saying is that worry and fear have never solved a single problem. Yet we habitually reach for it with our attention as if it were some universal panacea. I have found giving my attention to the truth that sets me free allows me to attend to life's details and challenges in a much more balanced and empowered fashion than worry or fear.

Each person decides with their free will what they will give their attention to. Each person takes accountability for what they are building a monument to with their love. I'm not saying live in denial or put your head in the sand. Give the outer world its due. Teach your children well. Eat and live responsibly. Pay your bills. But do not give your power away to anything limited.

If you find yourself tyrannized by the re-creation of limitation, fear and lack.... create a new response to these old tired limitations. You are God Consciousness. There is nothing limited about you. The purpose of your life is to experience yourself as beyond any limitation. The best most balancing focus is to give your attention to what sets you free.

11) **How does this work in the creation and maintenance of fulfilling relationships?**

Everyone here is equally Divine Love, equally God, equally sacred and holy. How you treat others is how you treat God. How you relate to yourself is how you relate to God. Treat others with the same respect and dignity you wish to be treated with.

Do not give your power away. If others are abusing you, harming you, treating you as disposable, value yourself. Create healthy boundaries; respect the divinity you have been given stewardship of. Trust that others are capable of healing themselves and if they are disrespecting your divinity, move on and do not let other's love of limitation define your understanding and acceptance of yourself.

12) *Wisdom Rising* **is the title of your third book. It is also a fabulous spiritual volume written almost for "deep wisdom on the go." What was your inspiration here?**

People asked me to write a book with shorter chapters that stood alone. That way if they didn't have a lot of time to read or if they put the book down for a week or more, it would not be a problem. They would enjoy each chapter independently as its own nugget of wisdom that would raise the quality of their life.

People also asked for stories from my own life that

enabled me to self-resurrect. People wanted easy to read and digest wisdom without short changing them on the depth and quality of the liberating knowledge that is in *"You Are What You Love."*

13) **Your radio shows are very popular due to your keen intelligence, sharp wit and ability to speak in-depth on a wide range of subjects. What aspect of radio do you find the most gratifying?**

You forgot to mention my humor. Just kidding.

I can support and help an unlimited number of listeners in improving the quality of their lives from the inside out and that is personally and spiritually satisfying. When I talk to one caller and break down what they are doing with their love and examine what is holding their suffering together, I am speaking to everyone listening about how to reframe their perspective on whatever the lesson or challenge may be and to ultimately feel better about their lives and why they are here. Human suffering is a very universal phenomenon. Everyone likes to think their suffering is unique and special but the reality of the matter is suffering is ubiquitous and inherent in the lives of all unenlightened beings.

I give individual, personal sessions. However as you can imagine there is no way I can sit down with every person on the planet, one at a time, before I die. With radio, and as an author, I can reach an unlimited number of people and I can continue to be of service long after my human experience has expired. And if I'm like Dannion Brinkley, and have 9 lives, I can keep coming back and extend the shelf life of my mortality. How good is that!

14) **Along with your radio shows and public speaking engagements, you conduct Self-Emergence Sessions. What can a client expect to gain from scheduling an appointment with you?**

I have had intuitive abilities since I was a child. Whatever you most need to understand about your life purpose and what you are doing with your love is what comes up in a session.

Everyone who makes an appointment gets whatever they most need to understand about why they are here, what their spiritual strengths are and how they sabotage themselves.

Imagine you had the opportunity to talk with your liberated mind, while the ego waited out in the hall. That is what these sessions are like.

15) **Do you have a formula for helping people find their purpose in life?**

Understand the law, you are what you love and you love whatever you give your attention to.

Remember that all life's challenges are working for you because you are the senior force of love.

Know that you cannot create a learning experience you do not need.

Everything is a sacred gift for you to claim that you can *BE LOVE NOW!*

16) **You are also an expert dream interpreter. You write about the dream work documented by Emmanuel Swedenborg in the 18th century. Would you share some of what you learned from his work regarding the significance of dreams?**

Swedenborg says that when we dream Angels come to us and speak to us in a symbolic, feeling/knowing language that is constantly commenting on the quality of our love.

So if you want to know what the Divine has to say to you about your life, and what you are giving your love to... listen to your dreams.

17) **Vaishāli, one of your most charming quotes is, "Whatever is worth doing is worth overdoing!" And you believe that choosing life "outside the box" is the only way to grow. Can you give me an example of how you suggest we can start to climb outside the box?**

A lot of people limit themselves because of what they fear others might think or say about them. If you want to try something like skydiving or writing poetry but you find your family may not approve or may be critical, choose to grow beyond those limited responses. Where would rock and roll be if Buddy Holly let others convince him rock music is of the devil?

Maybe you would like to dress differently or go join a ghost-hunting club but are afraid of what your friends, co-workers or neighbors would say. Don't waste your time living within other people's comfort zones. In other words, dress like Cindy Lauper or Lady Gaga when you sign up for the next paranormal field trip.

Fear is very confining and forces us to live in highly limited quarters. Living inside the box translates to not taking the risk to write the book you always longed to or not taking up painting because you are afraid people will look upon you as "not good enough." Or maybe it is something like not learning surfing or polka dancing even if you have always wanted to, because you were concerned others would laugh at you. Living inside the box is letting fear hold your life hostage. At the end of your life all that will matter is: did you have fun, did you play, did you explore what adventures your imagination invited you to?

The bottom line is this, and you know what the bottom line is… it is the little line at the bottom… when it comes to living "outside the box" the basic rule is a quote from James Dean, "Dream as if you'll live forever, live as if you'll die today." And Vaishāli's Rule of Conduit: If it isn't your problem, don't make it your problem. Just get out there and rock on, babies!

18) **What is your take on the galactic shift in consciousness we are now experiencing? Do you sense that the monumental energy surrounding the year 2012 is something we should all take note of?**

I see where you are going with this question, and yes, I do feel more profound and dramatic shifts and changes are coming. However, I am a real "here and now" present moment kind of wild woman. To me being present as a conscious force of love and choosing in every moment to give my attention to what is unlimited in nature is the only game plan I need, regardless of what year it is.

Tomorrow is promised to no one. I trust 2012 will take care of itself. Right now I am concerned with what am I doing with my attention now, in this present moment. The future is colored by how we relate to the present. The future is an extension of how we relate to each "now" moment. I feel the best way to honor the heightened opportunity for self-realization that is about to open to each and every one of us, is to make our mind our friend now.

I do not feel 2012 is about remaining loyal to limiting habits. So, I am focused on putting down whatever does not work for me now, so that when that time does come, I will walk into that new energy free and clear because I have valued practicing that in the now. Beam me up!

19) What is the Wild Woman's secret to living a happy, successful life?

If the truth be known… and I can tell you… Bugs Bunny is my religious symbol. He reminds me to not take reality seriously, to give all my enemies a kiss on the lips and to ask good questions like, "What's up Doc?"

Also any day I get up, and I do not have to talk to a lawyer or a doctor, and I can watch my religious symbol, I've cornered the market on happiness and success.

In the end, everyone's life is only as happy and successful as what they have chosen to give their attention to. And with that said may I suggest, "What's Opera, Doc?" a classic Bugs Bunny cartoon, or as I like to call it "animated enlightenment."

20) What personal dreams do you still aspire to manifest?

To love to the best of my ability. To remain a faithful and loyal resident of Heaven unconditionally. To go to as many Grateful Dead concerts as possible. To work like I don't need the money. To dance like I was at an endless Grateful Dead show. And, of course, to have plenty of organic, dark chocolate on hand. And when I die, I want Bugs Bunny to greet me on the other side. How cool would that be!!!!!

Heaven Can't Wait, Or How I Earned My Wings In The Mile High Club

*W*hen you are a Spiritual teacher, you know intellectually that no one ever dies, so you show up for life fearlessly. The body may give out but the Spiritual identity, the essence of a person, cannot, will not ever cease to exist. It is timeless and immortal. As the human embodiment of Divine Love, I cannot create any learning experience I do not need. Anything that touches my life here on Earth appears for one reason only... it facilitates my growth and expansion. Therefore I can release any regrets, unburden any sense of remorse and just get down to the business of getting the most out of this lifetime.

All of this works great in theory but the hard part has always been the practical application. How can I be sure that this enlightened wisdom is a knowing that extends beyond merely an intellectual storing of data? How can I be sure I have completely embodied this truth, taking it beyond the gray matter of the brain? How can anybody, for that matter, be sure they are not mentally deluding themselves with intellectual visions of self-imagined Spiritual grandeur? Right relationship with one's

Divinity must be lived, not just an action isolated to collecting frontal lobe facts and information. Even a bookshelf can accumulate vast canons of factoids, none of which, however, extend beyond the shelf they reside on and permeate into the whole of real life.

Little did I know when I boarded a plane for Puerto Vallarta, Mexico with my companion, Elliot, and his business partner, Stephen and wife, Kristin, that I would find myself entering a Spiritual Twilight Zone. I was soon to find myself in a first class seat to an unscheduled destination, an inner place of naked honesty, independent of what my brain knew to be true, before continuing on to our final destination in Mexico.

The flight started out routine enough. After a beverage, the flight attendants passed around a lunch of turkey sandwiches and potato salad. Elliot and I both laughed when he joked that he hoped that the pilot and copilot where not eating the potato salad - every bad airplane film he had ever seen always ended up with the cockpit crew dying of food poisoning from eating the potato salad, leaving no one to fly the plane. We continued to joke that it would certainly be a cruel death if it turned out *this* was in fact our last meal... and we didn't touch the potato salad.

The flight was smooth, not a bit of turbulence, and the bright blue sky seemed to promise that a trip to sunny, warm Mexico was just the ticket for a cold January vacation. After the lunch plates had been collected and we had just passed out of US air space, the unthinkable happened. It started out simple enough. The chief purser got on the intercom and asked if there was a doctor on the plane. Nothing too unsettling. After all people get sick on planes all the time.

As fate would have it there were four doctors onboard including a heart specialist. Elliot and I were in the third row, so we had a clear view as the purser opened the door to the flight deck and the line of doctors entered the cockpit. Next the purser asked if anyone onboard knew how to fly a plane. Elliot and I looked at each other and Elliot said, attempting to lighten the moment, "That's not good. I guess the crew really *did* eat the potato salad. I've already seen this movie! I wasn't thrilled about the ending either."

Planes are cramped quarters at best and the most surface area to lay a person out was in the first class galley. Elliot and I watched the doctors pull the captain out and lay him on the floor as a flight attendant ran past us with the onboard defibrillator. We watched the copilot move over into the captain's seat as the doctors worked intensely on the captain's immobile, prone body.

As this was going on, the four private pilots on the plane including Elliot's business partner, Stephen, had gotten together to see who was best prepared to copilot a 757, not an easy transition from the small propeller models these pilots traditionally flew. It turned out Stephen was the man. We watched him walk nervously by us, stepping over the captain's apparently lifeless body to enter the flight deck. As the minutes clicked away we felt the plane bank hard to the left, returning us back into US airspace. The purser announced that we would be making an emergence landing at the McAllen Airport.

After about five to ten minutes I felt a profound energetic shift. It was a feeling of freedom and great expansiveness. I turned to Elliot and asked, "Did you feel that?" "Feel what?" he answered. "The captain... he just died... I felt him leave. It was actually quite beautiful, very peaceful and loving." The doctors continued to work on the captain for the remainder of the flight back to Texas, although it was clear the man was gone. The purser then asked if there were any nurses on board. And again, as fate would have it there were four nurses, who rushed up to be of assistance.

It was a long thirty-minutes back to McAllen. The captain had just died right in front of our eyes and now the next challenge was the actually landing. McAllen Airport is not designed to land a commercial jet of this size. We were going to be pulling a big dog in on a short leash. People around us were understandably upset. No one panicked or screamed or made a scene. I could hear some people behind me quietly sobbing and praying. It was hard to tell if the emotion was for the dead captain or the anxiety about a potentially tricky landing, or a combination of the two.

Elliot and I had been talking about how accidents are usually the result of a variety of unexpected elements that come to-gether. We knew the copilot-turned-pilot was perfectly capable of landing the plane by himself. With the computers on planes these days, the planes actually land themselves under normal cir-cumstances. But these were not normal circumstances. It was not hard to imagine that the copilot might be just a tad distracted by the fact that his co-worker had just suffered a massive coronary and suddenly slumped over the controls, dying right before his eyes. We were now going to attempt an emergency landing on a runway not long enough to accommodate our plane.

Elliot suddenly turned to me and asked, "Are you okay with all this?" "Yeah," I said, "I'm surprised how totally and completely relaxed and calm I am. You and I know we can't die, so I'm okay. If it turns out that we just move on to the next phase of our existence without a body, instead of vacationing on the beach in Puerto Vallarta, I won't feel cheated. I suspect that God has a lot more work to get out of my butt, so I feel confident that everything will be just fine. But let's just suppose for a minute that I am over-estimating my importance in God's plan and that it really is time to punch the ticket and return home... I'm really good with that. You know," I told Elliot very sincerely, "I'm really grateful we are on this plane and getting this 'keep it real' experience because it is showing us that we have fully integrated what we know Spiritu-ally. *We live it.* It is not just a superficial, intellectual condition. The truth, we know, is embodied and it is comforting and strengthen-ing, and yes, liberating, experientially being able to claim this was well worth the price of admission." Elliot remarked, "I knew we shouldn't have prepaid for the rooms!"

The mind can have a nasty habit of lying to us. If I had been telling myself that I was at peace with the unfolding events, yet at the same time noticed I was white-knuckling it or on the verge of tears like those around me, I would have known the mind was not telling the entire truth. But the body was not tense or stressed in any way. The physical and emotional feedback all confirmed full disclosure. My emotional body was keeping it real. The well-practiced habit of identifying with my Divinity as pure love was officially senior to my fear of any physical mor-tality. This experience was bringing me the validation that real mastery had taken place, that my relationship with the truth had in fact set me free. Here I was on the same plane as every-one else, yet I was not having the same experience as everyone else. Knowing that I cannot die was and remains more real than whatever the world can throw at me.

I have a motto: if the wisdom you have is not pulling your butt out of the fire, then it is meaningless. If the inner guidance that you operate from is not empowering your movement through life, it is nature's way of saying, "Let it go." The good news is that it is never too late to make a liberating upgrade. You will know you have embodied the truth, because it will set you free. And you will know if you are investing in illusion, because it will not set you free. No one is immune to life's many firestorms. They have a way of finding you, inviting you to keep it real. Every experience in our lives occurs because it offers us vital wisdom that serves us.

This plane trip gave me the opportunity to claim the knowledge that I needed to know, in an arena I could not fake: that my relationship with my immortality was real and not just mental masturbation. The touchdown and landing went smoothly - executed with textbook precision. Instead of the usual landing where the plane slowly taxies up to the jetway, our plane came screaming up to the gate, finally coming to a complete stop right in front of the building. The passengers exploded in applause and shouts of relief and gratitude.

We remained at McAllen Airport another five hours or so, as local and federal officials examined the plane and took statements from the crew. The crew, by the way, could not have handled the situation better. They were all the picture of professionalism. The heart specialist who treated the fatally ill pilot told us he learned that this was the dead man's first day as a full captain. He had just been promoted. Since no one can create a learning experience they do not need, this man Spiritually required the experience of being made captain before his life's mission was complete. No one can go before their time. As it turned out, the flight attendant with the defibrillator had recently lost her son. I am sure this event was especially emotional for her. But she handled herself so well, no one without prior knowledge of her life would have been able to tell. In situations like these there is also a tangible post 911 maturity - we know how to focus ourselves and work together for a greater purpose.

At the airport, Stephen and his wife were sitting at the bar, she was getting a well deserved drink, when I asked him if it was exciting, as a private pilot, to have had the opportunity to land a 757? "Oh, yeah, sure, real exciting," Stephen said sarcastically as Kristin squeezed a lime into her beer. "First I have to step over a dead guy to get in the cockpit, now suddenly I have over two hundred lives on my hands I didn't five minutes before, and I'm at the controls of a commercial jet instead of my Cessna. Real exciting. Just how I wanted to start my vacation!" Stephen said to make matters even more stressful, the cloud cover was so low, he could not see the ground until an instant before the plane actually touched down. Stephen went on to explain that the planes voice activated computer system was announcing the landing time. It started with a minute, thirty seconds till touch down, Stephen could not see the ground at this point. Then one minute to touchdown, still no ground visibility. Finally when the computer announced thirty seconds till touchdown and still no sight of the runway, Stephen turned to the new pilot and said, "The computer's joking, right?" I can only imagine what was going through the pilot's mind when he had to explain, "No, Stephen, the computer doesn't make jokes. We are sitting two stories high, not five feet off the ground like in your plane." Elliot pointing out the upside to whole drama remarked, "But Stephen, this will look really good on your résumé." Everyone laughed.

During the many hours we all spent sitting around the McAllen Airport waiting to continue our journey to Mexico, we all had time to process the event. Many people were concerned about the captain's family, and what they would be going through. I heard several women talking about how terrible the captain's death was. Being a Spiritual teacher, I felt I could offer more helpful insight on the subject, so I offered a different point of view. "I know it is always shocking and unexpected when someone just drops dead in front of you, especially when it is the captain of the plane you're on, but let's really examine this. All of us will die some day. It is not of matter of 'if,' but 'when'. This man died doing what I presume he really loved. He did not suffer long. He got immediate medical attention so his family does not have to wonder, if this had happened at home, and if the ambulance had gotten there sooner might he have lived? As a matter of fact he could only have gotten faster medical treatment if this happened in the emergency room of a hospital. He did not have a heart attack on the freeway on the way to work, possible killing other people. He crossed over surrounded by over two hundred people who were wishing him well and praying for him and his family. I only hope that when my time comes, I manage to exit as graciously as he did. After all, we were on our way to Puerto Vallarta, Mexico. He was already half way to Heaven. And how many people can say when they crossed over they were still in a body for the first 30,000 feet of their ascension to the other side?"

Does This Human Experience Make My Spiritual Butt Look Big?

*E*veryone has heard the expression that we are Spiritual Beings having a human experience. However, remarkably few understand what that really means, and even fewer can incorporate the concept into their everyday lives. For example, women in particular are in the dark about what this means when it comes to being in right relationship with their body image. Whew! Just looking at those words "body image" is enough to send the average Earth Goddess into an uncontrollable crying jag. If we are Spiritual creatures having a human experience, wouldn't it make sense that we would approach this "body image" thing from a Spiritual perspective first, and from an anatomical agenda second? Yeah, right! How many women that you know are asking, "Does this make my butt look big?" because they are identifying with themselves Spiritually?

So how did this happen? How did we get all turned around and start putting the human cart before the Spiritual horse? When did the human tail start wagging the Spiritual dog? It happened the way most things claim their origin... it started with our perception. If Lily Tomlin is correct, and reality is little more than a collective hunch, then that collective guess began based on some perception ~ how we see the world, or in this case how we see ourselves. We habitually do not look in the mirror and recognize our Spiritual identity staring back at us. When we inspect our reflection, it is the carbon-based form in front of us that becomes the singular, myopic point of our focus. That is the tricky part about having a human experience. It comes complete with five sensory organs that override everything else. The physical world has a very nasty proclivity for getting right up in our faces, like a child begging for attention. Whatever we see, hear, feel, taste, or smell has a tendency to distract us to no end, supplanting what is not immediately seen, heard, felt, tasted and smelled, such as our Spiritual, physically invisible nature.

All of our attention zeros in on that extra weight we cannot seem to shed. Those horrible wrinkles that creep in no matter how many botox parties we attend. The bad hair cuts, the short eyelashes, the blotchy skin, the crooked teeth, the boobs that are either too big or too small, and the list goes on and on. Suddenly without realizing it, we have become a highly critical human being having a deeply dissatisfied present moment experience, completely void of anything even remotely Spiritual. The temporal, limited, human portion of the program has without question, completely over-shadowed the primary, unlimited, eternal Spiritual presence. Welcome to another day in paradise.

What would life look like if we could reverse that? How would the dreaded "body image" perception change if we viewed our Spirituality foremost, with more than the same intense scrutiny we normally apply to the physical? In order to answer that question, we must first understand and accept our Spiritual identity. It was the 18th century Swedish scientist / inventor / mystic, Emanuel Swedenborg, who pointed out that the source of all our unhappiness, depression, anxiety and disappointment with ourselves stems from our not knowing who and what we really are. We are not seeing ourselves as Spiritual Beings first, who are presently learning by adopting a human experience second.

Swedenborg is in the Guinness Book of World Records for having one of the largest IQ's. In a recent study by Stanford University he was acknowledged as one of the most brilliant people to have ever lived. Clearly, the man is more than qualified in his viewpoint. Swedenborg wrote over 35 volumes on the Spiritual nature of human beings and how our perception affects our relationship with our Divinity, our Spiritual identity. What Swedenborg says is that we have allowed the physical world to eclipse our attention from the greatest and most profound truth about ourselves, that we do not have Divine Love, we *are* Divine Love. Love cannot be taken away from us. It is not earned. How can we possibly earn what we already are? Furthermore, Swedenborg says that as Divine Love, we are also value, power and worth, because when did Love ever lack value, power and worth? For women this is liberating news. Your value and power is not in your dress or bra size; *it is what you are.* Try and trump that Victoria's Secret!

If you have been struggling with weight issues, or if you are battling anorexia and/or bulimia, this is what you have come to the Earth and taken a body to learn. You are Divine Love right now, and no one and no thing has the power to change that. Your physical packaging can and will change, but you are not your body. You are Divine Love right here, right now. You came here to claim, own and embody your Divinity as Divine Love. What is getting in the way is that your perception of yourself is something other than Divine Love.

Here is where the whole human experience gets even more confusing. Your body listens to what you give your attention to.

More than that, your body reflects back to you what you are doing with your attention. Your attention is designed to recognize
your True Nature. Your awareness, ironically, is supposed to set
you free. And it does… when owned and operated correctly. But
when you give your attention to an inner dialogue that incessantly finds fault with yourself, your body will go out of its way
to give you that imperfection, because it is under the impression
that this is what you want. That is what you are obsessively focusing on, and that is what the body hears.

All body image challenges, whether stemming from too much or
not enough weight, all have the same origin. Whoever is looking
in the mirror is not seeing a force of Divine Love looking back.
The Spiritual Being got lost in the shuffle of the human experience. Imagine how different your life would look and feel if the
first thing you said to yourself when you became self-reflective
is, "I do not have Divine Love, I am Divine Love, and I will not
allow any other definition to come between my awareness and
my Divinity. This is my story and I'm sticking to it. I show up
as a force of Divine Love first, and then as a bag of protoplasm
second." When this inner narrative occurs, the body then replies,
"Okay this is what I am! I am Divine Love," and then goes about
reflecting that back.

So much of the excess weight people struggle with is held in
place by unresolved emotions created by misplaced perceptions.
How many times have you heard about someone who suddenly
lost a significant amount of weight when they finally let go of
their anger, grief or that job or relationship that was so dysfunctional? When we give our attention to holding on to anything
that is not aligned with our true Spiritual nature, we carry that
burden around in some form or another. If you have tried every
diet, sampled every weight loss pill and still find yourself car-

rying more than your Divinity, maybe it is time to go on the "I will only tell myself the Truth about my Divinity" weight loss and body balancing program. It has zero calories, all you have to exercise is your attention, and there are no gym fees or sweaty, stupid human tricks to perform. All you have to do is value yourself for the eternal Being of Divine Love that you are. That Being existed before your body did; that Being will exist long after the body has fallen away. All you have to do is refuse to pack any additional critical weight. You are a Spiritual Being having a human experience. You are not a defective, "less than", broken human being who has lost touch with their Divinity. After all, since you are really a Spiritual Being first, imagine how breathtakingly perfect you will look and feel when you drop the weight of that ugly human perception!

What would Socrates Do?
Die With Dignity Of Course!

*I*n his time Socrates was considered the wisest man alive. He was condemned to death in 399BC after losing his trial, and died from drinking hemlock. How Socrates died is equally as important as his life. When I say *how* he died, I am not referring to his actual ingesting of poison. I am referring to his attitude about death and dying. Socrates firmly felt that death is a journey to be embarked on with excitement, that it is inherently a positive and liberating event. A far cry from how we view death today. So frequently we of the modern more advanced age describe death as "losing a battle," as succumbing, as a failure. We cannot just accept it; we must fight it to the very end. I wonder what Socrates would say about our so called age of enlightenment?

The Eastern healing sciences, Chinese Medicine and Ayurveda, refer to death as the ultimate cure: a final culmination and resolution of all that ails one. I suspect this point of view is one that would bring a delicate smile to the face of Socrates. The notion that dying is as natural as being born, an action that can be embraced with as equal a mindset as living, is not common or popular these days.

I received the following email from a close friend recently, and it reminded me of the expression, "What would Socrates do?"

Hi Vaishali,

Forgive me in advance if this gets too heavy, yet, I felt you'd find it compelling to say the least...

Today my friend Kenar died of cancer. She chose an option that no one ever speaks about, which is taboo to write about, and to acknowledge as a cancer treatment option, our choice to die from cancer. Yes, simply put, "I have cancer, I am okay with it, I choose to do nothing and I choose to die if that is spirit's will." As I type such words, I can only imagine how many people's stomachs may churn because this option is NOT how we have been taught to exercise our free will and our options to heal.

Here is Kenar's story:

She was only 36. I met her a little over a year ago. She became one of my closest friends in Los Angeles. She came to me for what I thought was help except at the time I failed to understand that it was support, not help, she needed, so I would keep offering her cancer treatment options; I could get her an appointment with Dr. Simone in Boston or Dr. Burzinksi in Texas; her family had the money for treatment. Then she was in Turkey so I urged her to try apricot pits; a mutual friend had an infrared sauna and I sent her the mumsnothavingchemo link about the infrared sauna, I told her about Laura Bond and 'mum' and felt www.mumsnothavingchemo.com would help her; she read the blogs weekly. She was open to organic juice and vitamin C injections but never did anything else. At my urging she bought Seth David Chernoff's book, http://www.SethChernoff.com and Vaishali's books http://www.PurpleV.com. I even told her about an energy healer named Marilyn Chernoff www.drmarilynchernoff.com and hemp oil!!! She always thanked me for my kindness and friendship...

Being a PR person on the cutting edge of all these viable health and integrative health options with rare access, I couldn't understand why my friend wouldn't try any of them. Then I realized that there was another option, another choice... she didn't want to be "saved" or cured, she wanted to be free. Freedom – a word that not many people put in the same sentence as death until I thought about Patrick Henry's "Give me Liberty, or give me Death!" Going though any kind of cancer treatment unless it was administered by "spiritual will" was death to Kenar, not the transitioning of the physical body. Kenar had made the choice to sacrifice a long life to live a free shorter one. Could this really be? The more I pondered Kenar's choice to do nothing and die, the more I began to understand that cancer may have taken Kenar's body but never once did it take her life. Never once did she say, "I'm afraid" or "I'm going to die," but on the contrary she often said when asked, "I'm not getting chemo. I'm not cutting anything out of my body. I am not giving my body, my quality of life, or money away to a flawed system that may or may not work." Then she'd smile and say, "Cancer may kill me, but it will NEVER take away my freedom to be alive."

People often commented that these were thoughts of depression, or delusion or both speaking. I began to wonder? Did her thoughts cause her cancer? Did her different view of life and of death give her strength and freedom? Or did it lead to her physical death? I couldn't help thinking how emphatically western culture tries to preserve life, at any cost. Just look at all the health care options, products and choices we have to save or prolong a person's life. Yet Kenar chose to live with cancer, to be with it, to accept it like one would do gray hair, or a wrinkled face, or not having a cell phone or allowing their home to foreclose...

She died yesterday. She told Stephen she had nothing else to live for and achieved just about all she set out to do (not in a depressed way but in an accepting way. She was truly at peace with death). She often said she would much rather have a quick death than live a butchered life... In the end she told me that she sought out a friendship with Stephen and I because she felt we would support and love any decisions she made without judgment and that she knew our "suggesting and sharing" treatment options were not trying to force her but an expression of love, because in the end we supported her decision to just live in the moment.

Through Kenar we can ponder the essence of what freedom of choice truly entails. Kenar, RIP dear soul.

Love,

Aime

Before dying Socrates reminded his friends and family that they would not be burying him, just his discarded shell. The real Socrates had simply moved on. If we had a window into the afterlife, I would not be surprised at all to see Socrates and Kenar together laughing, talking, and enjoying long quality conversations about the nature of real freedom and what is good and true.

Other Books By Purple Haze Press:

You Are What You Love®
By Vaishāli

You Are What You Love is the definitive 21st century guide for Spiritual seekers of timeless wisdom
who have hit a pothole on the way to enlightenment and are searching for the answers to the big
questions in life: "Who am I?" and "Why am I here?"
Author Vaishāli explores mystic Emanuel Swedenborg's philosophy of gratitude and love. She expands this wisdom by associating it to traditional
sources including Christianity and Buddhism.
Through storytelling and humor, the focal point
of the book "you don't have love, you are love" is
revealed. A compelling read to deepen your understanding of Oneness.

Paperback, 400 pages, ISBN 978-0-9773200-0-4,
$24.95

You Are What You Love®, Book on CD
By Vaishāli

Also available on CD an 80-minute condensed and
abridged version of the 400-page book counter
part. Read by the author.

CD, ISBN 978-0-9773200-2-8, $14.95

You Are What You Love® Playbook
By Vaishāli

You Are What You Love Playbook is a playtime manual offering practical play practices to invoke play into action. Included is step-by-step guidance on dream work, a 13-month course in how to practice playful miracles, and a copy of the author's lucid dream diary. The perfect companion to *You Are What You Love*.

Paperback, 124 pages, ISBN 978-0-9773200-1-1, $14.95

Wisdom Rising
By Vaishāli

Sometimes wisdom is best served up like M&M candies, in small pieces that you can savor, enjoy and hold in your hand. So it is with Vaishāli's new book, *Wisdom Rising*. It is a delightful, sweet, and satisfying collection of brilliant articles and short stories, that like gem quality jewels, are a thing of beauty, and a joy to behold.

It doesn't matter what your background is there is something to appeal to everyone in this book. Vaishāli's trademark "out of the box" sense of humor and wild woman perspective runs rampant throughout the book. Whether she is talking about the Nature of God or simply poking fun at our own cultural insecurities and hypocrisies, Vaishāli raises the bar on laugh out loud Spiritual wisdom. The entertainment as well as the wisdom rises flawlessly together, inviting the reader to go deeper in examining and showing up for their own life.

Everything about this book from the cover to the cartoon illustrations that punctuate every story, screams playful, fun, witty, and what we have seen Vaishāli dish up before, which is the unexpected ... no wonder she is know as "the Spiritual Wild Child."

Paperback, ISBN: 978-0-9773200-6-6, $14.95

Wisdom Rising, Book on CD
By Vaishāli
This 4-CD set is the condensed and abridged version of the 285 page book counter part. Read by the author.

CD, ISBN 987-0-9773200-9-7, $19.95

Longinus: Book I of the Merlin Factor
By Steven Maines
Longinus follows the tale of Gaius Cassius Longinus, the Roman Centurion who pierced the side Jesus with his spear while the condemned one hung from the cross.

After that fateful day, Longinus escapes Rome and the priests who want to take the spear and its supposed power for themselves. Longinus follows the Centurion's life from his love for the prostitute Irena to his mystical studies with the Druids of Gaul. But it also reveals Longinus' profound spiritual awakening through his Druidic studies and the spear that speaks to him with the voice of Christ.

Paperback, 241 pages, ISBN 978-0-9773200-3-5, $14.95

Longinus: Book I of the Merlin Factor
By Steven Maines
This abridged audio version of the critically acclaimed novel, follows the tale of Gaius Cassius Longinus, the Roman Centurion who pierced the side of Jesus with his spear while the condemned one hung from the cross. Abridged Audio

Book (3 CD). As Read By Mark ColsonCD, ISBN 978-0-9773200-7-3, $19.95

Myrriddin: Book II of the Merlin Factor
By Steven Maines

In *Myrriddin: Book II of the Merlin Factor*, it is the 4th Century A.D. A young boy has found sacred relics of the early Christians in the ruins of an ancient Druid temple on the Isle of Mystery in Old Britain. For reasons beyond his immediate comprehension, the lad connects with one item in particular;the Spear of Longinus, the very spear that pierced the side of Jesus and allegedly holds the power of Christ. The boy's name is Myrriddin. The world would remember him as Merlin, the greatest Druid and Wizard of all time.

Paperback, 217 pages, ISBN 978-0-9773200-4-2, $14.95

Myrriddin: Book II of the Merlin Factor, Book on CD
By Steven Maines

This 4-CD set is the condensed and abridged version of the 217 page book counter part. Read by actor Mark Colson.

CD, ISBN 987-0-9773200-8-0, $19.95

Masoud: Book III of the Merlin Factor
By Steven Maines

Follow the tale of Liam Arthur Mason as he struggles with the reawakening of his spirit and hence the ultimate advancement of his being. Experience his reawakening through his sacred initiation into the Knights Templar and his partnership with their Muslim counterparts, the Hashishim Knights, as well as through his passion for the woman Najeeba. And, finally be with him as he comes to fulfill his true destiny with the Spear of Longinus and Great King's Sword. Liam Arthur Mason was his Christian name. Masoud is who he would become.

Paperback, ISBN 978-0-9773200-5-9, $14.95

Geraldine Goodkitty
By F.J. Kercher

The author experienced a curious dream about a stray cat with the odd name Geraldine Goodkitty and her three kittens. She decided to write about each of the characters in the dream in order to probe its meaning. Geraldine's story began to expand, and the author continued to write. The story grew into a composite inspired by the wonderful animals that have graced her life and lent their names, personalities, and physical appearance to most of the characters in the novel. Geraldine's tale is told primarily from a feline perspective. However, the animal and human stories interweave at various points and eventually converge.

Paperback, 236 pages, ISBN 978-1-935183-05-1, $14.95